NO PHONEY WAR

BRITAIN'S PART IN THE SECOND WORLD WAR
3 SEPTEMBER 1939 - 9 APRIL 1940

NO PHONEY WAR

BRITAIN'S PART IN THE SECOND WORLD WAR
3 SEPTEMBER 1939 – 9 APRIL 1940

STEPHEN FLOWER

AMBERLEY

First published 2011

Amberley Publishing
The Hill, Stroud
Gloucestershire, GL5 4ER

www.amberleybooks.com

British Library Cataloguing in Publication Data.
A catalogue record for this book is available from the British Library.

ISBN 978 1 84868 960 2

Typeset in 11.5pt on 13.5pt Sabon LT.
Typesetting and Origination by Amberley Publishing.
Printed in the UK.

Contents

FOREWORD

The cinema screen was gigantic, filling an entire wall, and by its side stood a young man in a khaki drill uniform with Stetson hat, his serious air added to by the holstered gun on one hip. Less than three months since 9/11, and if the Twin Towers could fall anything was possible.

In the steeply inclined rows of plush seats the audience was tense. Sixty years after the event there was among them a sprinkling of grey heads whose owners were only too well aware of what they were about to see. The screen filled with a shot of the harbour's blue water, filmed by a helicopter skimming low over its rippled surface. Then the film changed to black and white, to jerkily focused shots of American battleships under attack. A grainy shot of high-flying Japanese aircraft, then a colossal explosion that seemed to shake the building.

In a subdued mood we filed out through a side door, to board the boat that would take us to the scene of the events we had just witnessed. White-uniformed sailors cast off and we turned to cross Pearl Harbor. Surely only the Hawaiian islands could be so sunny and beautiful on a December morning.

It had long been my ambition to visit Oahu, and sixty years after the attack that had brought America into the Second World War had seemed as good a time as any. I stepped onto the white metal floor of the Memorial, read the names on the far wall, then watched as one of my companions took the purple and yellow lei from round her neck. Bouganvillea and hibiscus petals floated across the shimmering water. From it protruded rusty metal and pools of purple oil broke the surface, floating away like jellyfish. Beneath loomed a vast dark shape.

This shrine marked the grave of the battleship USS *Arizona* – a ship that had been the pride of the US Navy and whose loss had been felt in homes across America. The survivors said that when the last member of her company died the flow of oil would stop.

Our tour group were almost the only Britons there that day. Few others could have known of another battleship, also lost to a surprise attack in a large anchorage surrounded by islands – a naval base that in 1939 had also seemed a long way from trouble. This ship too is a war grave, yet there is no cinema, no sightseers' boats and no memorial on the spot apart from a green wreck buoy, which bears a plea to divers not to disturb the crew's final resting place.

This ship is HMS *Royal Oak*, and she lies at Scapa Flow in the Orkneys. Her fate is part of that strange seven-month period that most Second World War histories gloss over. It was called the Phoney War, during which ships were sunk, aircraft were lost and men died. This is their story.

NEVER AGAIN?

The greater the lie, the more likely it is to be believed.
Adolf Hitler

Sunday 3 September 1939

Like that unforgettable Friday in 1963 when news came that President John F. Kennedy had been shot, everybody alive on this date would remember where they were when the outbreak of the Second World War was announced in Britain. Even though the build-up to this moment had been coming for years, its final confirmation would be vividly imprinted on their minds.

On that warm early autumn morning, friends and neighbours had drawn together, many inviting those who did not have 'the wireless' into their homes for the first time – a change from that usual standoffishness and desire for privacy that is part of the English character. Television, transmitted by the BBC at Alexandra Palace in North London from 1936, had ended just two days before, the plug being pulled in the middle of a Mickey Mouse cartoon. Not that this mattered too much, for its output had been restricted to those living within 40 miles of London. The bulky wooden cabinet with a small screen, receiving just one channel in black and white, would remain silent until June 1946.

So it was back to clustering round the radio. At ten o'clock the introduction was made by Alvar Liddell, using the calm, clipped tones taught by the BBC's pronunciation and enunciation class.

> This is London. The following official communiqué has been issued from 10 Downing Street. On September 1st His Majesty's Ambassador in Berlin was instructed to inform the German Government that unless they were prepared to give His Majesty's Government in the United Kingdom satisfactory assurances that the German Government had suspended all aggressive action against Poland and were prepared promptly to withdraw their forces from Polish territory, His Majesty's Government in the United Kingdom would, without hesitation, fulfil their obligations to Poland.

In Berlin the diplomats' families had already gone. Their German opposite numbers had left Croydon airport in a Lufthansa airliner during the last days of August. At 9 a.m. on the morning of 3 September, the British Ambassador, Sir Nevile Henderson, discharged what he must have known would be his final duty before departure. The Prime Minister would broadcast to the nation at 11.15 a.m.

In London the weather was breezy, with white clouds. A large but quiet crowd waited in Downing Street. Neville Chamberlain entered the Cabinet Room. Liddell, who leaned over him to make the announcement, noted that his shoulders were hunched and he looked 'very, very serious'. As Big Ben chimed the quarter hour, Liddell intoned, 'This is London. You will now hear a statement by the Prime Minister.' He was immediately followed by Chamberlain's sad, tired voice:

> I am speaking to you from the Cabinet Room at 10 Downing Street. This morning our Ambassador in Berlin handed the German Government a final note, stating that unless we heard from them by eleven o'clock today that they were prepared at once to withdraw their troops from Poland, a state of war would exist between us. I have to tell you now that no such undertaking has been received, and that consequently this country is at war with Germany.
>
> You can imagine what a bitter blow it is to me that all my long struggle to win peace has failed. Yet I cannot believe that there is anything more, or anything different that I could have done that would have been more successful.
>
> Up to the very last it would have been quite possible to have arranged a peaceful and honourable settlement between Germany and Poland, but Hitler would not have it.

No 'Herr Hitler' any more. What a contrast with the year before, when Chamberlain had stepped from his airliner at Heston airport, waving a piece of paper while proclaiming peace, to a relieved roar from those around him. A death sentence had been lifted, only to be re-imposed.

> We and France are today, in fulfilment of our obligations, going to the aid of Poland, who is so bravely resisting this wicked and unprovoked attack on her people. We have a clear conscience. We have done all that any country could do to establish peace. The situation in which no word given by Germany's ruler could be trusted and no people or country could feel themselves safe has become intolerable.
>
> It is evil things that we shall be fighting against – brute force, bad faith, injustice, oppression and persecution – and against them I am sure that the right will prevail.

The National Anthem was played, and in sitting rooms across Britain people rose to their feet. Scarcely had all this ended when the London air-raid sirens sounded a rising and falling note, which lasted for a minute.

People trooped obediently down into the nearest shelter entrance, some grimly wondering whether the piled sandbags by the door would do the job they were supposed to. Others grinned, took their places on whatever seats were available and, for once, exchanged a few words with strangers or muttered comments on Hitler's ancestry. Wasted no time, had he?

At the Admiralty, senior officers with gold-ringed sleeves and beribboned shoulders listened apprehensively as a series of heavy bangs sounded nearby, with comments like, 'My God, that was a near one.' Younger men believed them. Had they not survived Jutland and the rigours of convoy duty? People avoided one another's eyes while trying not to sound nervous or reveal what they were thinking. This was a sudden nightmare, even though they had been expecting it. Then the steady note of the all-clear sounded, sending them out into the afternoon sunshine.

There was nothing out of the ordinary. Buildings still stood and the traffic moved on, with no smoking ruins or ringing fire bells. The only sign that anything had happened was the silver-grey barrage balloons flying over the treetops. Not a single bomb had fallen. The Navy's veterans found, to their embarrassed relief, that the bangs had been caused by staff slamming a series of heavy wooden doors within the Admiralty building, to limit the spread of fire should one occur.

Rumour spread quickly. It was the Duke of Windsor, flying back to play his part. It was a French pilot who had omitted to file a flight plan. There had been a raid somewhere, with thousands dead and 'they' were trying to hush it up. Everyone knew that.

Nobody seems to have realised that there actually had been a German reconnaissance aircraft over London that morning. One of the photographs it took appears in this book.

What sort of a war was this going to be? Why had Britain gone to war over a country that most people had hardly heard of? Why, when, after 1918, the slogan, here and in France, had been 'Never Again!'?

*   *   *

This conflict had come about because of the desire, not just of one man, but also the nation he led, to avenge its defeat in the First World War. Adolf Hitler, leader of the National Socialist German Workers' Party, had been his adopted country's Chancellor since 1933. Himself a former frontline soldier, with the Iron Cross to prove it, Hitler lacked many human qualities, but nerve was something he had plenty of. Germany's post-war Weimar Government had lurched from one crisis to another, her once-proud army had been cut to 100,000 men, she was banned from having an air force, and her High Seas Fleet lay rusting at the bottom of the British naval base at Scapa Flow. Kaiser Wilhelm II had gone into Dutch exile, from which he would never return, and dreams of 'a place in the sun' had vanished when Germany's colonies had been taken from her.

The Treaty of Versailles had ended the war, then imposed huge reparation payments on Germany – a process which had descended into farce when most of the money had come from post-war American loans. A period of non-payment had resulted in French soldiers occupying cities in the Ruhr, Germany's industrial heartland, while treating civilians with contempt. The French General Foch had observed, 'The treaty was all a great pity. We shall have to do the same thing in another twenty years.' He would not live to see how right he was.

How was Germany to regain the world standing to which her population felt they were entitled? Follow Russia's example, and become a workers' paradise? It had nearly happened at the beginning of the 1920s, with Communist and right-wing mobs battling on the city streets. Racked by inflation and unemployment, patriotic Germans noted Soviet domination of the KPD, the German Communist Party. Increasingly, they looked to the Nazis, supporting Hitler because he told them what they wanted to hear.

From 1933 Germany slid into dictatorship. Trade unions were made subservient, other political parties were banned, and the brown-shirted *Sturm Abteilung* – the storm troopers – swaggered around the streets, noisy and arrogant. With them, and soon replacing many of them, came the apparatus of a police state. The SS, which had started life as Hitler's bodyguard, grew into a private army, with its own security service, the *Sicherheitsdienst*. Better known, though not uniformed, were the Secret State Police – the *Gestapo*. Germany would become cleansed and racially pure. Nothing binds people together like a common enemy, and blaming others for your own shortcomings is easy to do. It was made clear to the Jews that they were no longer welcome, and those who could began to leave.

For the average German, Hitler's accession meant more than fancy uniforms and torchlight parades. Unemployment is not hard to cure if you employ skilled men to make armaments and unskilled ones to build the new Autobahns that began to cross Germany. The change was summed up by a poster showing a hand reaching up to grasp a falling hammer, with the single word '*Arbeit!*' Work! Here at last was a real leader, a man of the people, who made promises and then delivered them. Now the population had money in their pockets and more to look forward to. Gone was the emptiness of unemployment. The Nazis had given everyone a sense of purpose and a reason to hold their heads up.

The world watched, at first dismissing Nazism as a fad that the Germans would soon be sensible enough to discard. Once that country was on its feet again – and it might be needed to curb any Soviet expansion – the strutting Brownshirts would disappear. Herr Hitler himself had served in the trenches, and been wounded twice. Surely he would not wish to start another war?

The answer lay with the German people themselves, without whom Hitler would have achieved nothing. While working in West Germany in

1977, I met a former British Army colonel who was then a civilian working for the British Army of the Rhine. He said, 'They're a strange people. Give them flags to fly, drums to beat and nice smart uniforms to wear, and they'll follow you anywhere.' This seems to be no longer the case, but it was certainly true in the 1930s. Few stopped to ask why.

Italy, gripped by Fascism since the 1920s, was also on the march. Its dictator, Benito Mussolini, pursuing dreams of recreating the old Roman Empire, launched an attack on Ethiopia in 1935. The League of Nations, a body set up hopefully to deter such aggression, listened as Haile Selassie, Ethiopia's Emperor, made a plea for assistance. Apart from deploring this affair, it did nothing – a fact that the Continental dictators, and others whose countries lay next door, duly noted.

The world seemed full of countries ruthlessly asserting themselves. In the nineteenth century, Japan had turned from a backward, inward-looking feudal society into a rapidly modernising country with imperial ambitions. The Germans had developed her army and – ironically – the British had built up her navy. In the early years of the twentieth century, the Japanese, without a formal declaration of war, had humiliated the Russians at Mukden and Tsushima. They had fought on the Allied side in 1914 but had withdrawn from the war after taking Tsingtao in China and several German-held islands in the Pacific. Unlike other nations, Japan had gained from the First World War, with few casualties.

Already the occupier of Korea and now with new footholds in China, Japan was on the move. Not yet an industrial giant and incapable of supporting her expanding population from her own resources, Japan cast greedy eyes around Asia. Manchurian coal and iron ore proved attractive, as did oil from Java, now being exported by the Dutch, but not in the quantities that Japan needed. Then there was rubber and tin, on British-owned plantations in Malaya.

Such expansion, if unchecked, would lead to clashes with other countries, among them Holland, Britain and the United States. Britain's Royal Navy, over half of it stationed abroad, might be needed for more than garrisoning the Empire.

China, saddled with a corrupt government, became a testing ground for the Japanese Army after an explosion on the Manchurian Railway in 1931 – an incident manufactured by the Japanese, as one of their surviving soldiers revealed in a television programme many years later. A bitter struggle lasted for over ten years, complicated by Chinese factions fighting among themselves until 1949.

In 1935 Saburo Kurusu, a Japanese diplomat, stated that foreign people did not know what it was all about, adding that it was Japan's destiny to lead oriental civilisation. Five years later, he would sign the Tripartite Alliance, tying Japan to Germany and Italy.

Luck seemed to run the dictators' way. The Spanish Civil War, fought from 1936 to the spring of 1939, gave Hitler an opportunity to try out his country's weapons. Already he had boasted that his new air force, the Luftwaffe, equalled the RAF. Now it was time to employ it. The Condor Legion, sent to Spain as 'volunteers', would successfully use, among other designs, the Messerschmitt 109 fighter and the Heinkel 111 bomber. New German tanks – another weapon forbidden until now – would give ground support.

With Germany now fully and for the most part enthusiastically under his thumb, Hitler began looking elsewhere. His friend Mussolini, whom he would later describe as 'Italy's greatest son', had tried his luck abroad and got away with it, so why should he not do the same? In March 1936, Hitler's troops marched into the Rhineland – an area 'demilitarized' after 1918. Britain and France did nothing. After all, why should the Germans not march into their own backyard? Other incursions two years later would be treated in much the same way. Appeasement was what mattered – giving Hitler what he wanted in the hope that he would not demand more.

The attitude of British and French politicians at the time may seem spineless now, but opposing Hitler meant rearming first, and there was little chance of an increase in military spending. Victory in 1918 had led to a complacent assumption that Allied weapons and tactics were superior. In any case, who was there to fight? In August 1919, the British Cabinet had announced, 'It should be assumed, for framing revised estimates, that the British Empire will not be engaged in any great war during the next ten years, and that no expeditionary force is required for this purpose.'

This Cabinet included Winston Churchill, then Secretary of State for War and for Air. To make matters worse, that ten-year limit was extended until 1932, acting as a brake on military expenditure until it was belatedly abandoned. Churchill had approved this renewal, although he would change his tune as future dangers loomed up.

The belief – the hope – during the 1930s was that the League of Nations could bring about a lasting peace through collective security. Should anything go wrong, the politicians could always blame the Service chiefs. In defence of those in government, by now they included men who had seen action in the trenches and for whom war's horrors meant more than names carved in Portland stone. Any effort, they argued, would be justified to avoid repeating such slaughter.

It was not only politicians who recoiled from the spectre of another war. At last British women had received the vote. Those without husbands or brothers, or who were now burdened with the care of disabled survivors, were not likely to support increased armament spending. Surely, education, housing and health mattered more. Anyone walking into a British city slum could see that. The threat of unemployment had been added to by the Depression.

An inevitable revulsion from war had led to an increase in pacifists, many of whom held the view that any future arms race would only provoke conflict, as in 1914. Cynical, conniving old men, with their conferences behind closed doors, were distrusted. Surely the League could offer something better than the old and discredited secret diplomacy. The Peace Pledge Union, with the slogan 'I remember war, and I shall never sanction or support another', grew to 400,000 members. Speakers at Hyde Park Corner, and the sight of prematurely old men walking with empty sleeves, had helped add to the numbers.

In 1933, the Oxford Union debated the motion 'That this house would in no circumstances fight for King and Country'. It was carried, and also noted by the dictators. Even as the clouds gathered in 1937, the pacifist philosopher Bertrand Russell thought the British would treat Nazi invaders as tourists: 'The Nazis would find some interest in our way of living, I think, and the starch would be taken out of them.' He apparently did not notice that the date was 1 April.

Britain had other preoccupations. If the sun had yet to set on her empire, its subject peoples were beginning to go their separate ways. Australia, Canada, New Zealand and South Africa had become self-governing Dominions – not automatically bound, as in 1914, to follow 'the Mother Country' into action in the future. India's Congress Party was calling for full independence, and planning began in the 1930s to envisage home rule for the subcontinent in the future.

In the meantime, Italy's aggression in eastern Africa could threaten British interests there, especially the Suez Canal. Japan continued to wage war in China, murdering 200,000 civilians in Nanking during December 1937 – an atrocity that shocked even the Nazis into attempting mediation. Britain's Services were stretched around the world, with no question of them being brought home to face some fresh European threat.

There was another reason for avoiding war. Aviation, spurred on by the First World War's technical advances, was beginning to shrink the world. Britain's aviation pioneers had led the way, from Alcock and Brown to Amy Johnson, who had become the first woman to fly solo from Britain to Australia. By the mid-1930s, converted bombers hopping across the Channel had given way to sleek silver monoplanes with retractable undercarriages and the first blind landing systems. For the ultimate in airborne luxury with a touch of romance, how about the Short C-Class Empire flying boats, off to Singapore and Australia?

However, aircraft that carried passengers one day could drop bombs the next. *The Shape of Things to Come*, written by H. G. Wells, prophesied a war in 1940 with Germany over the Polish Corridor – a strip of land under Polish control but with Germans living in it. This source of future conflict had come about following changes to Germany's eastern frontier after 1918. Less accurately, Wells visualised a twenty-year war, followed by plague and total dictatorship. His book was memorably filmed in 1936 with, for the time, some astonishing futuristic sets and special effects. 'Everytown', ruined by an unnamed enemy's aerial bombardment, was clearly London. Events in China, Ethiopia and Spain showed that modern war was not simply a matter of giving the school bully a bloody nose. Bombers could take it into everyone's backyard.

Could Britain expect any support from across the Channel? France was a weak and divided country, with street clashes between its left- and right-wingers. The French Army, weakened by wartime losses even worse than Britain's, was no longer the formidable force it had once been. Within the Third Republic, cabinets rose and fell, some lasting only a few hours. The birth rate also declined, with no more children sired by those who lay in mass graves from the Marne to Verdun.

If war returned, Britain would not be attacking Germany alone, but this time there would be no question of the next French generation going over the top to endure yet another storm of shot and shell. André Maginot, a legless former Army sergeant, had become Minister of Pensions, doing much on behalf of his fellow 1914–18 veterans. In 1929, by now France's War Minister, he put all his energy into a system of new concrete defences along the Franco-German frontier. It was the French press that applied his name to this line. He was determined that France's old enemy would not cross her borders again.

As for America, this country too was just emerging from the Depression. Its citizens, tired of European problems, had turned away from them after 1918. Some of their best young men lay beneath French soil, and for what? Europe was a mess that their forefathers had left behind. If another war came, they would stay out of it this time. Franklin D. Roosevelt, America's President, was seeking another term, but the next election was due in 1940. Any attempt to go against isolationism would hand the White House to his opponent.

For most people in Britain in the 1930s, Hitler was a far-off noisy nobody. This bellicose little man with his absurd moustache and his stray forelock was a gift to the newspaper cartoonists of the day. So was Neville Chamberlain, with his umbrella, wing collar and the manner of a nervous eagle. Churchill, with his pug face and turn-of-the-century taste in hats, was another. Politicians were seen as remote people in pinstripes. For the average family, it was more important to pass your matriculation, get yourself a job and hang onto it. A statement by Stanley Baldwin, then Prime Minister, that Britain's frontier was on the Rhine and that she must rearm to keep pace with Germany caused little alarm at first. It was still an era when people holidayed at home, making annual treks to Scarborough or Skegness, Blackpool or Brighton. Most of the young generation knew nothing of the Continent, and their fathers had no desire to return. Anyway, wogs began at Calais. Everyone knew that.

This attitude persisted when Hitler bullied Austria into an *Anschluss* with Germany in March 1938. So what if they were now united? They all spoke the same language. Matters showed more signs of coming to a head when Hitler threatened Czechoslovakia. This infant state, dating from 1918, had a number of Germans within its borders, living in an area known as the Sudetenland. Allegations of Czech mistreatment surfaced in the servile Nazi press, accompanied by 'refugees' sobbing on cue for the cameras. Hitler demanded the Sudetenland become part of Germany. He confided to Henlein, the Sudeten Germans' leader, 'We must always demand so much that we can never be satisfied.'

His tactics worked. Neville Chamberlain, now Prime Minister, flew to Germany three times to see Hitler. At Munich, in a conference that excluded the Czechs, Britain and France agreed to Hitler's demands. The border was opened, the Czechs conceded territory that included their fortifications, the Sudeten Germans greeted Hitler's troops, and Chamberlain, returning to Heston Airport, stated, 'It is the desire of our two countries never to go to war with one another again.' Knowing Britain was not ready for it, he had had no choice.

There are two versions of what Hitler said after Chamberlain departed. One was, 'He was such a nice old gentlemen, I decided to give him my autograph.' The other, which seems more likely, was, 'They have cheated me out of my war.'

Czechoslovakia, abandoned by those who should have been her friends, could do no more. Hitler declared that he had no more territorial demands to make, but few were surprised when his troops rolled into Prague, the Czech capital, on a snowy March morning in 1939. This was no welcoming back of Germans into the Third Reich's fold; it was an act of invasion. Still the rest of Europe did nothing.

Now it was Poland's turn. This country, sandwiched between Germany and Russia, had had an unhappy history, being repeatedly fought over and at times disappearing from the European map. The Polish Corridor, a route to the sea, severed East Prussia from the rest of Germany. The city of Danzig, though seen as free by the rest of Europe, was German but allegedly under Polish threat. Again, the atrocity stories were trotted out, with more tears shed on film.

That August, Hitler's hatred of the Poles, and contempt for their western allies, knew no bounds, as he addressed his military chiefs at his Obersalzberg home. 'Our enemies are worms. I saw them at Munich.' So had the rest of the world. Now he would need a pretext for the invasion of Poland.

> The victor will not be asked afterwards whether he told the truth or not. When starting and waging war it is not right that matters, but victory. Close your hearts to pity. Act brutally. Eighty million people must obtain what is their right. The stronger man is right. The greatest harshness.

Reinhard Heydrich, a senior SS officer, was an appalling, amoral individual intent on rising to the top of the Nazi tree. Already he was the heir apparent to Heinrich Himmler, the head of the SS, and there were rumours that he had his eye on Hitler's position. On 10 August, he had ordered SS-Sturmbannführer Alfred Naujocks to simulate an attack on Gleiwitz radio station, in Upper Silesia, near the Polish border. Heydrich commented, 'Practical proof is needed for these attacks of the Poles for the foreign press as well as German propaganda.'

The Poles were not angels – they had connived in Czechoslovakia's dismemberment, and anti-Semitism was strong among them – but there was little truth in the atrocity allegations. By now, the German people might have been expected to have seen through it, but extracts from the diary of Heinz Knoke, a future fighter pilot, make it clear that many accepted it without question. On 27 August he wrote:

> Our school becomes a barracks overnight, and the Armed Forces call up the Reserves. There seems to be a critical situation developing on the Eastern border of Germany and in Poland. Postmen are at work all through the night, hastening along the streets to deliver call-up notices and telegrams.

The atmosphere would have been like that notorious scene early in the film of *All Quiet on the Western Front*, where the old schoolmaster exhorts his pupils to leave their books to fight for Germany. This film had been a passionate plea for peace, all the more poignant because it was ignored. Erich Maria Remarque's book, adapted for the film, had been proscribed by the Nazis.

On 30 August, Knoke watched his friends depart:

> In the afternoon the first of our newly mobilized battalions is entrained at the freight depot. Trains are decorated with flowers as they leave for the front, but the faces are solemn. I recognise some of my classmates among them. The grim steel helmets contrast sharply with the youthful faces. Most of them I never see again.

The next day he added:

> The Polish atrocities against the German minority make horrible reading today. Thousands of Germans are being massacred daily in territory which had once been part of Germany. Thousands more arrive every hour in the Reich, each refugee with another tale of horror.

At 12.30 on the 31st, Hitler issued Directive No. 1 for the Conduct of War:

> Now that every political possibility has been exhausted for ending by peaceful means the intolerable situation on Germany's eastern frontier, I have determined on a solution by force. The date and time of the attack are now fixed: 1st September at 4.45 a.m.

This war would begin with lies and be sustained by them. As if the alleged atrocities had not been enough, the one planned at Gleiwitz now went ahead. At eight o'clock on that final August evening, five men in Polish uniforms attacked the station, locking up and guarding the duty staff. Those listening to a relay from Radio Breslau heard an apparently Polish voice, claiming to represent the 'High Command of Polish Volunteer Corps of Upper Silesia'. He claimed Gleiwitz was now in Polish hands and called on local Poles to rise up, promising that Danzig and Breslau would be Polish again. After four minutes of this, shots were fired in the air.

To give the attackers' charade some credibility the *Gestapo* had arrested Franciszek Honiok – a Silesian German, known for his Polish sympathies – dressed him to look like a saboteur, then killed him with a lethal injection. His body, with gunshot wounds added, had been left at the station for the press to view, as proof that the Poles had attacked it.

Not content with this, further attacks were staged by 'Polish' soldiers and others at nearby Pitschen and a customs post at Hochlinden. Six concentration camp inmates, dressed as Poles, were drugged, then shot. Again, their bodies were left by the building. Heydrich had given them the cynical codename of 'Canned Goods'. No one seemed to ask why there were no German casualties from this surprise attack.

On this night, Hitler made his intentions plain to Nazi officials:

I have issued the command and I will have anybody who utters but one word of criticism executed by firing squad – that our war aim does not consist in reaching certain lines but in the physical destruction of the enemy. Accordingly, I have placed my death's-head formations in readiness, with orders to send to death mercilessly and without compassion men, women and children of Polish derivation and language. Only thus shall we gain the living space that we need.

The clock ticked on into the early hours of 1 September. At 4.17, some eager Germans in Danzig began firing on Polish positions. At the correct time, the old battleship *Schleswig-Holstein*, supposedly on a goodwill visit, fired on a nearby Polish garrison. At 5.40, all German radio stations broadcast Hitler's declaration:

The Polish state has refused the peaceful settlement of relations which I desired and has resorted to arms. Germans in Poland are persecuted with bloody terror and driven from their homes. A series of violations of the frontier, intolerable to a great power, prove that Poland is no longer willing to respect the frontier of the Reich. In order to put an end to this lunacy I have no choice but to meet force with force; the German Army will fight for the honour and rights of a new-born Germany.

The Second World War had begun.

The end of Hitler's speech on 1 September. (IWM Neg. No. HU39976)

2

FIRST BLOOD

I shall never start a war without the certainty that a demoralised enemy will succumb to the first stroke of a single gigantic attack.

Adolf Hitler

Backed by their breaking of the German Enigma code – for which Britain would later owe them a great deal – the Poles had prepared Plan Z, the defence of their country against attack from the west. They did not expect to hold out indefinitely, but hoped to do so for six months, until Britain and France had intervened.

Their position was unenviable. Poland consisted mostly of a flat plain, with the Carpathian mountains to the south. Several rivers crossed it, but in late summer these could be easily forded. A rural and backward country, the Polish landscape consisted of strip farming, with an appearance similar to that of Britain in the Middle Ages. Retreating into the country's centre would mean abandoning much of its population and industry to the invaders.

The Polish Army was its country's pride, with its best recruits going to the cavalry. However, it had not undergone the trench warfare of 1914–18, and consequently the drive for mechanisation that had taken place elsewhere had been slower. The army was outnumbered two to one and short of modern weapons, while its armour consisted of light tanks and tankettes, which would be totally outclassed by heavier German vehicles. Its artillery, almost entirely horse-drawn, was under strength, dating back to the First World War.

On top of all this, during August the Poles had faced diplomatic pressure from Britain and France to postpone mobilisation for fear of provoking Hitler. The result was that units were still assembling when the Luftwaffe arrived overhead. Polish airmen were not wiped out on the first day: with a characteristic sense of survival, many of their 392 available aircraft had been dispersed, thus surviving the first attacks. However, Poland's obsolete and outnumbered squadrons did not seriously threaten German command of the air for long. Use of Slovakia as a satellite had lengthened the German border around Poland, resulting in thrusts from the north, west and south. The Poles fought furiously, throwing some attacks back, but these were repeated until successful.

Although a detailed study of the Polish campaign is outside the confines of this book, one legend deserves to be rebutted. On the afternoon of 1 September, two squadrons of a Polish cavalry unit, the 18th Lancers, attacked and literally cut to pieces a German infantry battalion in a clearing. As they did so, some German six-wheeled armoured cars arrived, opening fire on the Poles as they galloped for safety behind a nearby hillock. A cameraman filmed this as it happened, and it did indeed look as if the Poles had taken part in a suicidal charge. Italian war correspondents saw the carnage the next day and were told by German soldiers that the Poles 'had charged the tanks'. So the legend began.

German armoured spearheads rolled deep into western Poland, the metallic thunder of tank tracks at times drowned out by an eerie howl from overhead. The angularly ugly Junkers Ju 87B dive-bomber, with sirens mounted on its undercarriage, attacked roads, communication lines and marshalling yards. Heavier bombers followed, targeting over one hundred Polish towns and cities on that first day. Polish troop losses were high, and movement was made difficult by fleeing civilians clogging roads. The German minority turned to sniping and fifth-column activities, giving the Poles an excuse – as if one had been needed – to turn some of the atrocity stories into fact.

Hitler's non-aggression pact with the Soviet Union the previous month had stunned the world, clearing the way for all this. Under a secret agreement within the pact, the Red Army crossed Poland's eastern frontier on 17 September, splitting the country in two. Ten days later, Poland's battered capital, Warsaw, surrendered.

It was not only the Poles who would be marked out for special treatment. There was no Final Solution yet, but it was coming. Two months later, Hans Frank, now the German Governor-General in Poland, said to his administrative heads, 'We won't waste much time on the Jews. It is a joy to finally be able to physically attack the Jewish race. The more that die the better: to strike him is a victory of our Reich.'

British and French assurances had been to no avail. Those Poles who had not escaped or been murdered by the SS now disappeared into a black nightmare that would last for five years, during which an estimated 7 million of them would die.

*   *   *

As the Poles fought, the debate in Britain continued. On 1 September, the Cabinet ordered its initial preparations to go into operation. With fears of an apocalyptic air raid dominating everything, the evacuation of children to the country began. In London the Smithfield meat and Billingsgate fish markets were decentralised. The blackout was imposed that evening. Those with memories of 1914 recalled Sir Edward Grey, the then Foreign Secretary, saying, 'The lights are going out all over Europe. We shall not live to see them lit again in our lifetime.' This time, Chamberlain was among those who would never do so. Heavy dark curtains were hung over outer doors and windows. Those who owned cars now had to provide masked headlights, then paint mudguards and running boards white.

That afternoon Winston Churchill arrived at 10 Downing Street, at Chamberlain's invitation. This had been reluctantly given, as the Right Honourable Member for Epping had been out of ministerial office for ten years and, ever since the Gallipoli fiasco in 1915, had been looked on as a dangerous adventurer. His warnings about Hitler's intentions had been scorned and he had unwisely backed Edward VIII during the Abdication Crisis in 1936. Churchill was now in the position of someone whose opinion of Hitler had been proved right, among other men, including Chamberlain, who had been appeasers. From Chamberlain's point of view, bringing Churchill into the War Cabinet would silence a critic. Better to have him in the tent than plotting outside it.

Seeing no hope now of averting war, Chamberlain proposed a War Cabinet of ministers without departmental responsibilities. The Labour Party was unwilling to join a coalition, but Chamberlain hoped the Liberals would. Churchill accepted the invitation, but urged that Anthony Eden, the former Foreign Secretary, be given a post, to which Chamberlain agreed.

That evening in the House of Commons Chamberlain said, 'We shall stand at the bar of history knowing that the responsibility for this terrible catastrophe lies on the shoulders of one man. The German Chancellor has not hesitated to plunge the world into misery to serve his own senseless ambition.' There was a feeling of sympathy for him as he read out the warning that Sir Nevile Henderson had been instructed to deliver to Joachim von Ribbentrop, Hitler's Foreign Minister.

That evening both Henderson and the French Ambassador, Robert Coulondre, arrived at the Foreign Ministry in the Wilhelmstrasse to hand their warnings to von Ribbentrop. These were passed on to Hitler, who derisively said, 'We will now see if they come to Poland's aid.' He opined that 'they'll chicken out again'.

Stations in France were by now full of soldiers, refugees and evacuees. At Berlin's Stettiner Bahnhof the scenes were similar, as blue-tagged children queued for trains. Edouard Daladier, France's Prime Minister and another architect of the Munich Agreement, was given a standing ovation in the Chamber of Deputies when he said that French obligations must now be fulfilled. An Italian peace conference proposal was rejected; but it was stated that if the Germans withdrew, the British Government would regard the situation as it was before the attack.

To the Opposition and to many of those behind Chamberlain, this looked like a last-minute attempt to back out of Britain's obligations. In a hostile atmosphere Arthur Greenwood, the acting Labour leader, said, 'I wonder how long we are prepared to vacillate at a time when Britain and all that Britain stands for, and human civilisation, are at peril … The moment we look like weakening, at that moment dictatorship knows we are beaten. We are not beaten. We shall not be beaten. We cannot be beaten, but delay is dangerous.' He was cheered by all sides.

Sensing an imminent revolt, Chamberlain and Sir Kingsley Wood, another appeaser, met those within the Cabinet who had stepped out of line. His pleading that the problem was synchronising the British ultimatum with the French one was met with the reply that he should make it regardless of the French. He agreed, if necessary, to act alone. A warm day ended with an appropriately heavy storm over London.

On 3 September there was a feeling in France that the Poles were going to be abandoned, as the Czechs had been. Despite Daladier's attitude, there were those in the Chamber of Deputies who saw Communism as a worse enemy, and who would join the collaborationists less than a year later.

Henderson now handed a final ultimatum, with the eleven o'clock deadline, to Doctor Paul Schmidt, Hitler's interpreter – an action he particularly regretted, as Schmidt was a popular member of Berlin's diplomatic community.

At 9.20 that morning Schmidt arrived at the Reich Chancellery in Voss-Strasse. Hitler was in his office with von Ribbentrop, who stood by the window as if in anticipation. After Schmidt's translation, there was silence. Hitler asked, 'What now?' to which von Ribbentrop replied, 'I assume that the French will hand in a similar ultimatum within the hour.' He was correct – not that it took much working out. Schmidt informed Hermann Göring, the Luftwaffe chief, and others in the anteroom. In the stunned silence that followed, Göring said, 'If we lose this war, God have mercy upon us!' The worms had finally turned.

Showing ignorance of the British character and admiration for its Empire, Hitler launched into a tirade:

> The Poles are a miserable, good-for-nothing, loud-mouthed rabble. The British understand that as well as we do; the British gentlemen understand that might is right. When it comes to inferior races, they were our first schoolmasters. It is disgraceful to present Czechs and Poles as sovereign states when this rabble is not a jot better than the Sudanese or the Indians – and only because on this occasion it is about German interests and not British ones. My entire policy towards Britain has been based on recognising the natural relations as they exist on both sides, and now they want to put me in the pillory. That is an unspeakable vilification.

After Chamberlain's radio announcement, the House of Commons sat on a Sunday for the first time since George III's death in 1820. By now a few MPs were in uniform. Chamberlain, hardly an inspiring figure, vainly hoped that he would live to see 'a restored and liberated Europe'. Sir Archibald Sinclair, the Liberal leader, praised the determination of the French people, while Churchill summed up the war's aims as only he could:

Outside the storms of war may blow and the lands be lashed with the fury of its gales, but in our own hearts this Sunday morning there is peace. Our hands may be active, but our consciences are at rest ... This is not a question of fighting for Danzig or fighting for Poland. We are fighting to save the whole world from the pestilence of Nazi tyranny and in defence of all that is most sacred to man. This is no war of domination or imperial aggrandisement or material gain: no war to shut any country out of its sunlight or means of progress. It is a war, viewed in its inherent quality, to establish, on impregnable rocks, the rights of the individual, and it is a war to establish and revive the stature of man.

That evening Churchill took up his former post of First Lord of the Admiralty. The signal 'Winston Is Back!' went out, to the cheers of the Royal Navy.

Someone who had once worn an Admiral of the Fleet's uniform was not so enthusiastic, and, like those waverers in the Chamber of Deputies, saw a worse threat lurking behind Nazism. The Duke of Windsor, who had chosen exile and marriage to Wallis Simpson after abdication, had waited anxiously at a villa in the south of France. Now, after a phone call from the British Ambassador in Paris, he told the Duchess, 'Great Britain has just declared war on Germany, and I'm afraid in the end this may open the way for world Communism.'

Someone else who opposed Britain's entry into the war was Sir Oswald Mosley, leader of the British Union of Fascists. A First World War veteran who had become an MP, he had crossed the floor between the Conservatives and Labour before turning his back on both to form the BUF, accompanied by others of his generation who bitterly remembered unkept promises about a land fit for heroes to live in. His party's black-shirted members had clashed memorably with left-wingers in London's East End in 1936. Their slogans included 'Fight To Live, Not Live To Fight' and 'Britons Fight For Britain Only'. His message to the BUF on 1 September is worth quoting in full, if only because it illustrates that anti-Semitism was not confined to central Europe:

The Government of Britain goes to war, with the agreement of all the Parliamentary Parties. British Union stands for peace. Neither Britain nor her Empire is threatened. Therefore British Government intervenes in an alien quarrel. In this situation we of British Union will do our utmost to persuade our British people to make peace.

Before war began, in our struggle for peace, our thousands of members had awakened great masses of the British people to demand peace. But sufficient of the people could not be awakened in time without the money which we did not possess. The dope machine of Jewish finance deceived the people until Britain was involved in war in the interest of the Money Power which rules Britain through its Press and Parties. Now British Union will continue

Chamberlain leaves 10 Downing Street after announcing war. (IWM Neg. No. HU5538)

its work of awakening the people until peace be won, and until the People's State of British Union is born by the declared will of the British people.

To our members my message is plain and clear. Our country is involved in war. Therefore I ask you to do nothing to injure our country, or to help any other Power. Our members should do what the law requires of them, and if they are members of any of the Forces or Services of the Crown, they should obey their orders, and, in every particular, obey the rules of their Service. But I ask all members who are free to carry on our work to take every opportunity within your power to awaken the people and to demand peace.

We now enter a period when the people will be roused by events. When we have awakened sufficient of the people to the truth, peace will be won and Britain and her people will be saved for a glorious future.

To this mission I shall continue to devote my life. Nearly twenty-five years ago, when I was barely eighteen years of age, I was flying over the German lines in the last war. Later, I faced the Germany of the Kaiser in the trenches.

We have said a hundred times that if the life of Britain were threatened we would fight. But I am not offering to fight in the quarrel of Jewish finance, in a war from which Britain could withdraw at any moment she likes with her Empire intact and her people safe.

For the moment I am not concerned to argue about the incidents which preceded the outbreak of war. In time we shall know the whole truth.

It is sufficient to say that a war cannot be fought every twenty years to prevent any remedy of the injustices in the Peace Treaty which concluded the previous war.

I am now concerned with only two simple facts. This war is no quarrel of the British people; this war is a quarrel of Jewish finance. So to our people I give myself for the winning of peace.

Mosley received little sympathy. Most people, whatever their politics, were resolved to fight Hitler, but how? There was no question of racing single-handed across Germany to Poland's rescue. Britain's island status had meant a large navy and a small army. Like 1914–18, this war would have to be a combined effort, but with whom?

On 3 September, Franklin D. Roosevelt proclaimed America's neutrality, but made it clear where his sympathies lay:

I hope that the United States will stay out of this war. I believe that it will. And I give you assurance and reassurance that every effort of your government will be directed toward that end. As long as it remains within my power to do so, there will be no blackout of peace in the United States.

The pioneering airman Colonel Charles Lindbergh's speeches in support of isolationism were widely applauded. Also in favour, for different reasons, was the Bund, the American Nazi Party, drawn from German-Americans who resented fighting against their homeland.

In early 1940 the British Ambassador would report that nine out of ten Americans wanted to avoid war, feeling strongly that Britain was trying to drag them in. With America determined to stay out, for Britain France would serve as an ally and as a forward base. While her army was being rebuilt, any contribution Britain could make would have to be at sea or in the air.

Shortly after Chamberlain's war announcement, a Bristol Blenheim of 139 Squadron took off from RAF Wyton in Huntingdonshire, its task being to reconnoitre the German port of Wilhelmshaven. It had been decided, for fear of provoking massive retaliation, that land targets would not be attacked, especially civilians in towns. Depending on the circumstances, Bomber Command would attack any ships in the harbour, but not if they were in the dockyards – there was too great a risk of bombs falling on land.

The Blenheim's crew included a Royal Navy commander – apparently in case its pilot was unable to recognise an enemy warship – and flew at 24,000 feet, taking 75 photographs but being unable to communicate as its radio had iced up – the first of a series of equipment failures that were to plague the RAF throughout that first wartime winter. They found the German fleet leaving harbour, apparently in anticipation.

The primary reason for the RAF's existence as a separate force was the doctrine of strategic bombing: wearing down an enemy's morale and his means of making war. Now, with the role of its bombers circumscribed, what was it to do? On that first night ten Whitley bombers flew over Hamburg, Bremen and other cities. Thick cloud over north-western Germany hid them, and there was no opposition apart from a few searchlights. Their bomb doors opened and over 5 million propaganda leaflets fluttered down. The text gave a truthful account of why Britain had gone to war, stating that they had no enmity with the German people, whom the British felt had been deceived by the Nazis, and that they would be happy to end hostilities with any future peace-loving government.

These leaflet raids would continue for some months to come, and the use the Germans made of the paper is easy to guess. Although the Air Ministry's thinking at this time was full of errors, assumptions and false expectations, they had had the sense to realise that the Whitley, the oldest and slowest of the RAF's bombers, was unfit for daylight operations. At least their crews gained valuable night navigation practice over a blacked-out country.

One 58 Squadron Whitley became Bomber Command's first casualty. Having taken off from Leconfield in East Yorkshire for a 'Nickel' raid (as these flights were codenamed) to the Ruhr industrial area, it suffered an engine failure. The next morning it force-landed in a field near Dormans, on the River Marne in France. Remembering the episode in a television interview thirty years later, the pilot said, 'We jerked to a halt with cabbages flying past the window!' Some entered the bomber, but there were no injuries.

Loading leaflets into a 102 Squadron Whitley. (IWM Neg. No. C912)

Dispensing leaflets from a Whitley. This shot was posed on the ground – at altitude, gloves were essential to avoid frostbite. (IWM Neg. No. C826)

1. Jahrgang Nr. 6   Luftpost-Ausgabe

WOLKIGER BEOBACHTER

Sonderausgabe für Österreich.

Anschluss.

Österreich im Krieg.

Österreicher! Ihr steht im Krieg gegen England — im ersten Kriegswinter. Deutscher Imperialismus zwang Euch in diesen Krieg gegen das englische und das französische Weltreich, und Ihr könnt nur verlieren.

Warum?

Deutschland führt Krieg, um alle die Grundsätze der Freiheit endgültig zu vernichten, für die Ihr einst gekämpft habt. Selbst wenn Deutschland gewinnen würde, was gar nicht möglich ist,—Ihr könnt nur verlieren.

Für Ribbentrop sterben?

Hitler spricht von einem langen Krieg, und Deutschland muß einen langen Krieg verlieren. Sollen Österreicher sterben und leiden, um die Blödheit Ribbentrop'scher Ambitionen zu beweisen, und damit die SS. ihre Uniformen in Warschau spazieren tragen können?

Eine Waffe.

Es ist noch nicht lange her, seit wir unsere Visitenkarten, mit den guten Wünschen der Demokratien, in Österreich und Böhmen abgegeben haben. Unsere Grüße bringen Euch eine Waffe,—die den deutschen Machthabern in Österreich mehr Angst einflößt, als jede Andere:—

Die Wahrheit.

Diese Zeitung, die aus den Wolken zu Euch herabflattert, ist von Goebbels nicht zensuriert. Sie schreibt, was die Außenwelt denkt, und bringt Euch Nachrichten, die Euch verheimlicht, oder nur in verdrehter Form zugänglich gemacht werden.

Unsere Zeitung erzählt Euch auch, was die Nazis Euch nie erzählen werden, nämlich, daß Ihr Frieden haben könntet . . . .

Kurze Nachrichten.

Daladier und Churchill haben beide in ihren Reden erklärt, die Wiedergutmachung des Österreich zugefügten Unrechts sei Ziel der englischen und französischen Politik.

Der Panzerkreuzer "Admiral Graf Spee" hat sich nach einer siegreichen — wohlgemerkt siegreichen — Seeschlacht selbst versenkt. Eine neue "Sonta"!

Der drittgrösste deutsche Handelsdampfer "Columbus" hat sich auch versenkt.

Der neue deutsche Langstrecken-Kampfflieger hat in englischen Pilotenkreisen wegen seiner Unzuverlässigkeit den Spitznamen "Klepper-Falt-Flugzeug" erhalten.

A leaflet dropped by the RAF, mimicking the *Völkischer Beobachter* and intended for Austria.

102 Squadron's Whitleys at RAF Driffield in East Yorkshire. Already the fuselage roundel's white ring has been reduced to avoid being highlighted by searchlights. (IWM Neg. No. C921)

Briefing at RAF Linton-on-Ouse in the Vale of York. This round-the-table scene would contrast sharply with the formal briefings of later years. (IWM Neg. No. CH219)

The inevitable jokes did the rounds. There was the pilot questioned about a late return. 'No, sir, I didn't drop them. I landed in Germany and went round posting them through the letter boxes.' Then there was the frustrated observer who admitted that, instead of cutting open the bundles, he had dropped them as they were, no doubt hoping a solid lump would do some good by descending on a Nazi head. His intelligence officer had been appalled. 'Good God, man, you might have killed somebody!'

Among Whitehall warriors the feeling was that it was all going rather well. The writer Compton Mackenzie, an agent in 1914–18, was told by an Air Ministry official, 'We are not going to drop bombs on Germany. We are going to drop propaganda leaflets. Don't you think that's a wonderful idea?' Those who burned the heart out of Hamburg some three years later would wonder at such attitudes.

If the RAF was having to fight without teeth, Churchill was determined that the Navy would do better, but how could it take the fight to the enemy? In 1939 Britain still had the largest navy in the world, with 15 battleships, 7 aircraft carriers, 66 cruisers and 184 destroyers.

Although some ships dated back to the First World War, this was a formidable force, born of a proud Service that had ruled the waves since Trafalgar. The only serious challenge had come during 1914–18, and the one big naval battle, off Jutland, had been indecisive, although British losses had been high. With the exception of a few ships that had been abroad at the start, the German High Seas Fleet had never reached the high seas. The U-boat – the German submarine – had proved more of a menace, but this too had been curbed and, as with the other Services, there was a tendency to believe that victory had proved their tactics to be superior.

It quickly became clear that while nothing might happen yet on land and little in the air, there was to be no lull at sea. On 1 September the liner *Athenia*, a 13,581-ton ship of the Donaldson Line, left the Clyde. Of over 1,000 people on board, 143 were Americans, which perhaps was the

The Queen Elizabeth-class battleship HMS *Malaya*, veteran of Jutland and typical of the Royal Navy's capital ships in 1939. (IWM Neg. No. A7734)

reason why dockyard workers yelled 'Cowards!' at them as they left the dock. That said, some alarmed crewmen's wives had dissuaded their men from sailing.

The *Athenia* had the reputation of comfortable informality, and other passengers had been taken aboard, as several other voyages had recently been cancelled. On 3 September, after picking up further passengers from Liverpool and Belfast, she headed for Montreal, now with many more Canadians, Americans and European refugees on board. Of these, thirty-four were Germans, some of them Jews.

As dinner was served that evening, the liner was blacked out. The war's outbreak reached them via the radio station at Valentia in Ireland, and the skipper, Captain James Cook, put up a notice. The passengers quietened down, especially the younger ones, some of whom had a premonition of disaster. All twenty-six lifeboats were made ready, two being swung out, with some rafts also being available, providing ample space for everyone.

Commodore Karl Dönitz, the head of the Kriegsmarine's U-boat arm, signalled, 'U-boats to make war on merchant shipping in accordance with operations order.' The *U-30*, commanded by the 25-year-old Oberleutnant Franz-Julius Lemp, headed for its operational area.

In 1935 Germany had signed the London Treaty of 1930, which limited submarine warfare. Permissible targets included troopships, those carrying war materials, or any ship escorted by enemy warships or aircraft. A U-boat captain could also stop and search any ship deemed hostile by the uncovering of guns or the transmission of signals enabling the Royal Navy to locate him.

At seven that evening, *U-30* was on the surface when Lemp spotted the *Athenia*. He suspected her to be an armed merchant cruiser – a liner fitted with guns – and dived fifteen minutes later. He was unsure of the ship's identity but suspicious that she was zigzagging without lights, even though daylight was now fading. At 7.30, for the first time since sailing, Captain Cook joined the first-class passengers for dinner – which was seen by most of them as a good omen. On deck some children entertained other passengers by singing 'South of the Border, Down Mexico Way' – a popular hit of the day.

On a night like this some First World War veterans could not resist playing the old soldier. In the first-class dining room one of them reassured the actress next to him that the Germans would wait until the ship came back with armament. Then the torpedo hit No. 5 hold, aft of amidships, on the port side, entering the engine room and wrecking the galley. Some people died never knowing what had hit them.

Lemp had fired four torpedoes, two of which had missed, while a third failed to leave its tube. The lights went out and the ship tilted, with passengers, crockery and furniture thrown to one side of the room. An SOS was sent, initially in code, reaching Valentia. A plain-language repeat read, 'SOS from British steamer *Athenia*. Posn 56 degrees 42 minutes N

14 degrees 05 minutes W torpedoed. 1400 passengers some still aboard sinking fast.' This was answered by the Norwegian freighter *Knute Nelson*, 40 miles away, which turned to assist, even though her captain doubted the torpedoing.

Survivors were to speak of a second explosion and thought the liner had been shelled as well, but this was probably due to Lemp's crew forcing out the malfunctioning torpedo with compressed air, causing it to go off after leaving the U-boat.

At 8.15 Lemp surfaced. Georg Hoegel, *U-30*'s radio operator, intercepted the *Athenia*'s signals, alerting Lemp to the fact that she had been unarmed. 'What a mess!' Lemp commented to his gunnery officer. An hour later the SOS was still being sent, with only two boats left to be launched. Apparently inspired by the *Titanic*'s legend, some passengers were singing 'Nearer, My God, to Thee' or 'Abide With Me'. One survivor saw *U-30* three hundred yards off the port bow.

By now the American freighter *City of Flint* and the yacht *Southern Cross* were on their way, the latter signalling: 'Distance from you 50 steaming full speed to your assistance.' After receiving a report that all passengers were off the ship, Cook changed into civilian clothes before following them – in 1914–18 the Germans had taken merchant captains prisoner.

The liner *Athenia*, the first British ship lost in the Second World War. (IWM)

At midnight the *Knute Nelson* arrived on the scene, followed by the destroyer HMS *Vanquisher*, with HMS *Vivacious*, her flotilla leader, to provide assistance. At half past two in the morning the *Southern Cross* followed, lit up like a Christmas tree, with her Swedish flag clearly visible. Her owner, Axel Wenner-Gren, the founder of Electrolux and an acquaintance of Göring, evidently hoped that highlighting her neutrality in such a manner would avoid further sinkings. In total, 380 survivors climbed aboard the yacht, with 430 rescued by the *Knute Nelson*. The liner's list to port had made launching the starboard lifeboats more difficult. One had fallen from its davits, throwing all on board into the sea, a second had capsized, and a third fouled the *Knute Nelson*'s screw when coming alongside.

The Commander-in-Chief Western Approaches directed three more destroyers to the scene. By half past four in the morning, HMS *Electra* and HMS *Escort* had arrived, with HMS *Fame* to follow. James Bass, serving on *Escort*, was one of several sailors ordered into the debris-littered water to assist survivors. Screaming women begged the sailors to save their children. One, trying to reach her dead baby, gouged his face with her nails. Orders had been given to leave bodies in the sea in order to concentrate on the living. Oil seeped into his scratches, resulting in excruciating pain and a bad skin condition. Another woman grabbed at his neck, making him fear for his life. Not surprisingly, he was to suffer nightmares afterwards.

Some survivors were landed at Greenock, others at Galway in Ireland. Their faces told of the ordeal they had suffered, with weary children peering from under thin blankets. Two Americans told their stories for the newsreel cameras. One woman broke down, unable to continue, but the other, a thirteen-year-old girl, was remarkably calm. The exact number lost remained uncertain. The press reported 112, but the Donaldson Line estimated the toll as 128.

Inevitably, the sinking was a propaganda gift to both sides, with the Germans denying responsibility. The *Völkischer Beobachter* claimed it had been a conspiracy started by Churchill, who had ordered the *Athenia* sunk. All this was reminiscent of the loss of the *Lusitania* in 1915, with the same accusations flying about. As had happened then, despite the loss of some of her citizens, America would stay out of the war for a further two years.

Believing unrestricted submarine warfare had been launched, Churchill pressed for a convoy system to be immediately instituted. Dönitz tightened his control over the U-boats, and in the immediate future most sinkings would occur among independently travelling merchantmen. From now until March 1940 U-boats would sink over 200 ships, of several nationalities, including neutrals, in the Western Approaches.

The Navy's answer to the submarine was Asdic, named after the First World War Anti-Submarine Detection Investigation Committee. It was an echo-sounding system, giving off a series of 'pings', which would be picked up from a submarine's hull. Asdic had limited range and could not pick up

Survivors from the *Athenia* land at Galway. (IWM Neg. No. HU51012)

a U-boat on the surface at night – a fact that skilled U-boat skippers would turn to their advantage when attacking convoys at that time.

The Fleet Air Arm had only recently been returned to Admiralty control and was still equipped with obsolete aircraft, most of them biplanes. The Fairey Swordfish would later win fame at Taranto, but the FAA ought to have had something better from the start. The Fairey Fulmar had the eight-gun armament of the RAF's Hurricane and Spitfire, but was a large two-man fighter with an indifferent performance, due to their Lordships' insistence that a pilot needed navigation assistance when at sea.

The Blackburn Skua, an uneasy compromise between a fighter and a dive-bomber, had taken time to come into service. It turned out to be underpowered and pilots found its controls heavy, fearing that it would spin if flown too slowly. Its cousin the Roc, a turret fighter, would be as much of a disaster as the RAF's Boulton Paul Defiant. Of the seven aircraft carriers, only HMS *Ark Royal* was modern and purpose-built: the others had all begun life as battleships.

The Navy expressed its power in terms of its battleships, though most were slow, dating from the First World War. However, the chances of another Jutland were remote. Germany's Kriegsmarine had been rebuilt from scratch in the interwar years. Although most of its ships were modern and its standard of gunnery excellent, the surface fleet had not been ready when the war began. Under the Z Plan, Germany would have built more surface ships and, if peace had been maintained, would have been in a position to challenge the Royal Navy on equal terms by 1944. Instead, Grossadmiral Erich Raeder, the Commander-in-Chief, knew, even if Hitler refused to listen, that his surface fleet was vastly outnumbered. He said, 'At best, they will die with gallantry.'

Instead, this looked like being the war of the submarine and the pursuing destroyer, armed with depth charges. For now, the only method of bringing a submarine to the surface, or sinking it, was to pass over it with the Asdic pinging. When the operator announced 'Instantaneous echo', over the stern went the depth charges, each too powerful to be fired ahead of the ship without sinking it as well.

One ship that would be in the thick of it from the beginning was the new destroyer HMS *Kelly* – a ship that during her short life would achieve fame, due in part to the talent of her captain for publicity.

Kelly had been one of the destroyers included in the Emergency Programme of Naval Construction for 1937. Built on Tyneside, she had been commissioned in August 1938 and was commanded by Captain Lord Louis Mountbatten. Few men had so many connections, related as he was to not only Britain's royal family but to others across Europe – as a child he had known Tsar Nicholas II as 'Uncle Nicky'.

Although a brave, hardworking, patriotic man, who was popular with most of those who served under him, Mountbatten was a conniving individual and a driven one, with a desire to win at all costs. His father, Prince Louis of Battenberg, had been the Royal Navy's First Sea Lord until hounded out in the middle of the First World War because of his German origins. His son's resentment never abated and he swore that one day he would hold the same office as his father – an ambition he achieved in 1955.

Now he commanded the 5th Destroyer Flotilla of eight ships. An innovator who had done much to improve fleet wireless telegraphy, Mountbatten had, almost inevitably, visited the naval architect's office with suggestions of his own while *Kelly* was taking shape. Her depot was at Chatham, where she took on the rest of her ship's company in the summer of 1939. Mountbatten addressed his crew, stating that a happy ship was his intention, then informed them that the process of taking on stores and ammunition, which normally took three weeks, would now have to be completed in three days! It was done, and she sailed for working-up trials off Portland.

Kelly was at sea when a warning came to fuse all shells and make torpedo warheads ready. Mountbatten was lecturing all officers and petty officers on the Stationkeeper – an invention of his that automatically kept the ship in station with others, enabling the officer of the watch to concentrate on other matters. Just as his lecture was ending, a petty officer handed him a signal, which he slipped into his pocket until he had finished. It read:

'From Admiralty to all concerned at home and abroad. Most immediate. Commence hostilities at once with Germany.'

Mountbatten's tone was unemotional. 'War has broken out.' They then heard Chamberlain's broadcast, followed by Mountbatten over the Tannoy. 'Whenever we leave harbour we shall be right in the face of the enemy, who will be out to destroy us. We must find him and destroy him first.'

The chance was not long in coming. While on an anti-submarine exercise with the destroyer *Acheron* and a motorboat, two torpedoes that were not dummies passed. All three ships went into action, the motorboat having Asdic as well. Both destroyers dropped depth charges and a large patch of oil surfaced, earning them a 'probable'. However, as there is no record of a U-boat being lost at this time, the oil had probably been vented through a torpedo tube by its crafty commander, who had then made good his escape while everyone on the surface was cheering.

Therefore, although useful, the Asdic system was not infallible. On 3 September the destroyer HMS *Walpole*, in Saint George's Channel, obtained what seemed like a good Asdic contact. The attack resulted in a shoal of dead fish! There was also a naval version of the RAF's leaflet jokes. A lieutenant-commander reported to the captain on a destroyer's bridge:

'The ship's engines have stopped, sir.'
'I know. There's an enemy U-boat about.'
'Are you going to depth-charge her, sir?'
'No. I'm sending a diver down with leaflets.'

If the Fleet Air Arm was not yet up to the job, what about the RAF? Coastal Command had been formed in 1936, but rearming at the eleventh hour inevitably meant that priority had gone to new fighters and bombers, leaving maritime reconnaissance as the Cinderella of the Service. Coastal Command began with an assortment of older aircraft, including obsolete biplane flying boats like the Supermarine Stranraer and short-range types like the Avro Anson – an aircraft with a leisurely gait, more suited to transport and training, with a small bomb load. Nearer the mark were the Short Sunderland flying boat and the Lockheed Hudson. Both converted from pre-war airliners, they were faster monoplanes with roomy cockpits and the ability to carry a heavier offensive load.

However, any aeroplane attacking a U-boat is only as good as the weapon it drops, and the delayed-action anti-submarine bomb turned out to be useless. The answer was to modify the Navy's Mark VII depth charge, but that would take time. Also, co-operation between aircraft and convoy escorts left much to be desired, due to stupid inter-Service disputes. The FAA had not accepted the RAF's assurances of protection, remained bitter at having been a poor relation for most of the interwar period, and argued that the best remedy was modern carrier-borne aircraft, travelling with the convoys, especially across the middle of the Atlantic, which no RAF aircraft could yet cover.

If U-boats could not be located, what about the enemy's surface fleet? On 4 September the pocket battleship *Admiral Scheer* lay at anchor in the Schillig Roads, off Wilhelmshaven. Part of the watch was on deck, while on the foretop platform the anti-aircraft officer, with a Luftwaffe counterpart, was looking through aircraft recognition tables. Then a loudspeaker barked, 'Three aircraft at six o'clock – course straight towards *Scheer*.'

The Luftwaffe officer immediately recognised them. 'They're Tommies – Bristol Blenheims!'

It was as well that he was there. As warning bells sounded, the first Blenheim, attacking at mast height, dropped two 500-pound bombs, which struck the deck, bounced and went over the side. There were no explosions. Light flak opened up on all three aircraft. Other bombs dropped by them also failed to explode. A second wave of three failed to attack, being thrown about by the flak and jostling each other as they ran in towards the ship. One took a direct hit and plummeted into the water, leaving an oily stain. The others disappeared into cloud.

A few minutes later, now facing alert defences, came another five Blenheims, targeting the light cruiser *Emden* and other warships. At this moment the cruiser was changing her berth, with tugs towing her away from the jetty wall. Bombs from one aircraft fell between the two, then this Blenheim, hit by fire from the heavy cruiser *Admiral Hipper*, dived in flames, hitting *Emden*'s bows level with the cadet quarters.

Next it was the turn of the battlecruisers *Scharnhorst* and *Gneisenau*, anchored off Brunsbüttel in the Elbe. Fourteen Vickers Wellingtons of 9 and 149 Squadrons went in, under attack from Messerschmitt Bf 109s. Two 9 Squadron bombers went down and their bombs hit nothing. Worse news had come when it was found that one crew, due to a navigation error, had bombed the Danish town of Esbjerg, over a hundred miles from the target, killing two people.

Out of twenty-nine aircraft involved, seven had been lost and others damaged. The only German losses had been a dozen seamen killed by the crashing Blenheim. Whether that had been accidental or a last defiant act by its pilot, nobody would ever know. If so, it pre-dated the Japanese *kamikaze* attacks by over two years.

The squadron adjutants at RAF Honington and Wattisham, in East Anglia, would have letters to write. 107 Squadron had lost five Blenheims and twelve men. Flight Lieutenant J. F. Barton and his crew were possibly the first Bomber Command casualties of the war.

Sergeant A. S. Prince did not come back either, but his observer and gunner, Sergeant George Booth and Aircraftman Larry Slattery, both did, after enduring five and a half years behind the wire. Booth would return to Horsforth, near Leeds, and be photographed giving his six-year-old son a present. He had last seen him as a baby.

9 Squadron's Wellington Mark Is. During late 1939 these were superseded by the Mark IA, with superior Nash & Thompson gun turrets. (IWM Neg. No. CH4)

Not only had the bombs failed, but the whole raid had been badly handled. 149 Squadron's crews had been kept hanging around for a day, with rumours that they would be going to Germany. They had discovered the target only after an inadequate briefing, given solely to the pilots.

Nobody knew where Brunsbüttel was, and old maps had to be checked to find out. There had been no time to study them before or form an attack plan. All they had been told was that there were two cruisers at the Kiel Canal's entrance. One Wellington had become unserviceable, necessitating a last-minute hunt for another, and Flying Officer Bill Macrae, a Canadian pilot, had nearly taken off without a bomb load – a fact he had discovered only by checking. Squadron Leader Paul Harris ordered his guns to be tested in flight, only to discover that none of them worked. On top of all this the weather was bad, with cloud over the Heligoland Bight almost at sea level, causing some aircraft to turn back without bombing.

There is a saying that no plan survives first contact with the enemy. This was the first of a series of lessons that would be painfully learned by the bomber crews, though initially not by those above them, over the coming months. That the crews found their targets at all seems a wonder. Things were conducted in so amateur a fashion that the massed night raids of the later war years, with complicated briefings, use of coloured marker flares and electronic navigation aids, would seem to come from another age.

Bomber Command were not the only ones facing a learning curve. On 5 September a submarine on the surface off the west coast of Scotland was surprised by a 233 Squadron Anson returning from patrol. As the Anson dived to attack, the boat quickly submerged, without recognition signals. Two 100-pound bombs were dropped so low that they bounced off the water. Since the impact had activated their fuses, both went off, puncturing the Anson's wing tanks. The crew then ditched in the River Eden estuary, off Shelly Point, took to their dinghy and were quickly rescued. It was believed that a U-boat had been sunk, but the mess celebration that followed was cut short when the Admiralty informed them they had attacked HMS *Seahorse*, without causing much damage.

Another submarine was not so lucky. HMS *Oxley*, of the Navy's 2nd Flotilla, had left Dundee on her first combat patrol, off the coast of southern Norway. The night of 10 September was dark and starless. It was then that *Oxley* strayed into an adjacent area, allocated to *Triton*, another 2nd Flotilla boat.

Spotting her on the surface, *Triton* flashed the correct recognition signal three times, followed by a recognition grenade. There was no response and *Triton*'s torpedo struck *Oxley* amidships, causing her to blow up and sink in seconds. Only her skipper and a signals rating escaped, the mistake being realised when they were picked up. Both captains were exonerated, as it was found that *Oxley*'s signal lamp and grenade projector had both failed.

German U-boat crews had their own problems, being handicapped by some defective torpedoes and the 3,600-mine barrage laid across the Channel, which sank three U-boats before they took the long way to the Atlantic via the North Sea. Hanging around off the Scottish coast did not produce good results either. After an unsuccessful attack on HMS *Ark Royal* on 14 September, *U-39* was crippled and her crew all captured by three destroyers.

They must have been surprised to be sent to the Tower of London, by now a Prisoner of War Collection Centre. The officers went to the officers' mess, with the men in barrack rooms. Interviews were conducted in the Old Hospital Block. Their stay was a short one, as they were sent north on 21 September, the officers going to the Officers' POW Camp No. 1 at Grizedale Hall in the Lake District – then the only one in Britain for them – and the men to Camp 127 at Oldham in Lancashire.

The Navy's primary weapons were convoy and blockade – the former bringing food to Britain while the latter, known as the Northern Patrol, was intended to deny it to the Germans. However, this would not be as effective as in the previous war. In 1918 Germany had been on the brink of starvation when the Armistice came. This time grain and oil were flowing easily along secure land routes from Germany's new ally, the Soviet Union, which was delivering promptly and in full measure. Provided Hitler did not antagonise Josef Stalin, it could continue for years to come.

Impatient for action and thinking himself a better strategist than the professionals, Churchill was not content with, as he put it, 'this defensive obsession', deciding to sweep the Western Approaches as an anti-U-boat measure. In putting together three hunting groups, each equipped with an aircraft carrier, he ignored the fact that the U-boat could achieve little without attacking the convoys.

The result was the near-loss of *Ark Royal*. On 14 September she picked up a distress call from the steam ship *Fanad Head*, which was being chased by a surfaced U-boat some 200 miles away, near Rockall. Three Skuas from 803 Squadron took off, armed with one 100-pound bomb and four 20-pound bombs under their wings, followed by six Swordfish from 810 Squadron. *U-39*, also in the area, was not picked up by the escorting destroyers' Asdic and fired two torpedoes, which were spotted by a lookout. The carrier turned towards them and they missed, one exploding harmlessly astern of her. Depth charges damaged *U-39*, forcing her to surface with the capture of forty-nine men before she sank.

It was *U-30*, of *Athenia* notoriety, that was pursuing the *Fanad Head*. Lemp had fired one shot at her. She stopped, he allowed her crew to use the lifeboats, then sent four men across to board her, salvage food, then lay demolition charges. Lieutenant Richard Thurston, a Skua pilot, attacked, but was too low. Bomb splinters set his Skua on fire. Thurston ditched, and although both men got out, he reached the *Fanad Head* alone. Suffering from burns, he was pulled aboard by one of the Germans.

Lieutenant-Commander Dennis Campbell, in the second Skua, then attacked what he thought was *U-30* under the surface. Signalling to the lifeboats that help was coming, he returned to the carrier. Lieutenant Guy Griffiths attacked, but also flew too low, ditching with a damaged rear fuselage. He too reached the *Fanad Head*, but also lost his gunner. Lemp then resurfaced, telling everyone to get clear as he was going to torpedo the ship, which broke in two after he had done so.

The boarding party and their two prisoners returned to the U-boat as the Swordfish were spotted. Despite their attacks, the U-boat escaped damaged. Lemp covered his tracks by not breaking radio silence to report the *Athenia*'s sinking. He subsequently landed a wounded man in Iceland – then a Danish colony and therefore neutral. Maschinenobergefreiter Adolf Schmidt received medical treatment in Reykjavik after he had sworn an oath never to mention the *Athenia*. Schmidt kept this up even when taken prisoner during the British occupation of Iceland in 1940, though after the war the truth emerged when he testified during the Nuremberg trials.

U-30's log page for 3 September was replaced by one showing false information in another hand, placing her 200 miles west of her actual position that night. After reporting his actions to Dönitz, Lemp was fully debriefed in Berlin. Instead of a court martial, which some would have thought justified, he rose to Kapitänleutnant and received the Knight's Cross the following year. He died during the capture of *U-110* in 1941.

Next it was the turn of HMS *Courageous*, off the south-west coast of Ireland. As with *Ark Royal* and *Hermes* in the other two groups, the idea was that the carrier would attract U-boat attacks, her four escorting destroyers then intervening with Asdic. This, it was intended, would distract the enemy from merchant ships. Two Swordfish squadrons, totalling twenty-four aircraft, were aboard. Sailing so far west of the Isles of Scilly meant no need for fighter protection, so none was carried.

It is worth detailing Fleet Air Arm flying procedures to show how primitive things still were at this time. Crews were summoned, in the best naval tradition, by a bugler blowing 'flying stations' on the Tannoy, from their wardroom to the crew room in the carrier's 'island' superstructure. Having changed into their flying kit, which with open cockpits they would certainly need, they then ran to their aircraft. On 17 September this took place at three o'clock in the afternoon for the squadron on standby, with only an hour until the other took over.

Pilots ran up to their bomb-carrying aircraft while the operations officer briefed the observers. They then boarded, carrying their navigation instruments and the Bigsworth board. This was a square wooden frame fitted with parallel rulers to which they clipped a chart. They would navigate with this on their knees. Facing aft was the telegraphist/air gunner, with a single Lewis gun – a First World War relic prone to stoppages. He also tuned the aircraft's W/T set to the carrier's frequency, keeping a listening watch. The TAG then attached himself to a 'jockstrap' – a safety wire that clipped onto the harness between his and the observer's legs. Communication between the pilot and observer was via the Gosport tube – primitive but clear.

Eight aircraft and two of the destroyers were now going to the aid of the liner SS *Kafiristan*, which was being threatened by a surfaced U-boat. *Courageous* altered course, increasing speed to 25 knots, but due to W/T silence could not inform the Swordfish. All the liner's crew and passengers were rescued by the two destroyers, which transferred them to another merchant ship. When the Swordfish returned, the final one was flown by Lieutenant Charles Lamb, on the last dregs of his fuel. He landed despite the batsman's attempts to wave him off.

It was now eight o'clock in the evening. As Lamb and his observer reached the wardroom, two of *U-29*'s torpedoes struck simultaneously on the carrier's port side. There was a sudden silence as the lights went out. Boats were swept from stowage below to be crushed by the flight deck's port side, the list being added to by aircraft sliding across the hangar. The ring main had been severed, cutting all power, meaning that the command to abandon ship could only be passed on after it had been shouted several times. Something – probably a mast aerial – fell across the funnel's siren lanyard, which gave out a mournful blast.

Discipline still applied. The Royal Marines fell in neatly on the sloping deck, waiting for their captain who, unknown to them, had been blown over the side. They jumped only after one of the FAA squadron adjutants bawled at them to do so. Some men fell 70 feet, including three reservists who were old and unable to swim. Lamb helped one to the destroyer *Impulsive*, but the man did not survive.

After twenty minutes the carrier went down, losing 514 men from 1,260. An escort, seeing *U-29*'s twin periscopes close to the carrier's stern, had attacked. Her depth charges missed the U-boat but killed several men in the water.

HMS *Kelly*, patrolling off Land's End, answered the SOS, though by the time she arrived the carrier had gone down. Some survivors were picked up by her. Others were picked up by two merchant ships and were then transferred using *Kelly*'s motor cutter.

Courageous had indeed done what Churchill had required: she had attracted a U-boat attack. The hunting groups were disbanded and the lessons of the First World War were belatedly recalled. In the meantime *Kelly* and her sister ships patrolled or escorted convoys. The demand for destroyers was now as high as it had been twenty-five years before, and 90 per cent sea time was not unusual. This was true of cruisers as well – on 16 September Boy Seaman 2nd Class William Crawford wrote in his diary

HMS *Courageous* sinking. (IWM Neg. No. HU53423)

aboard the new cruiser HMS *Belfast*: 'Still out at sea. I don't know where we are or where we are going to.'

On the 18th an incident occurred which boosted British morale. The tramp steamer *Kensington Court* had been en route from Argentina to Birkenhead with a wheat cargo. In the early afternoon, some 70 miles from the Isles of Scilly, Captain J. Schofield spotted a surfaced U-boat in daylight less than a mile away. He turned the ship stern on, but the U-boat closed the range, opening fire with her deck gun.

Schofield ordered his radio officer to send an SOS. This included the call GGG – indicating a gun attack. *U-32*'s skipper, rightly thinking that neither the Navy nor Coastal Command had enough resources to cover all areas, had attacked on the surface, saving his expensive torpedoes.

Four Sunderlands received the SOS, three from 228 and one from 204 Squadrons, the first to arrive being piloted by Flight Lieutenant Thurstan Smith of 228. The ship was down by the bows when he arrived, landing to pick up twenty of her crew.

This was not as simple as it seemed, for the flying boat's duralumin hull, one-sixteenth of an inch thick, had not been intended for landing on the open sea. Sunderland crews needed seamanship. Smith was close, but not too close to the boat, in case it damaged his aircraft's hull. The men were ferried over four or five at a time, using the aircraft's two dinghies with lines trailing behind it. Flight Lieutenant John Barratt of 204 Squadron carried out an anti-submarine sweep before landing to pick up the remainder.

Two months later Smith and Barratt received Distinguished Flying Crosses at Buckingham Palace. There was a thank-you of a different kind later when Billy Cotton's dance band recorded a patriotic ditty entitled 'Wings Over The Navy'. One version of it featured the voice of Captain Schofield, thanking Coastal Command for their rescue.

On 24 September, two days after *Ark Royal* had again avoided torpedoes, the submarine HMS *Spearfish*, taking part in the blockade of German shipping, was severely damaged by prolonged German destroyer depth charge attacks in the Kattegat. She evaded them and surfaced, but, being unable to submerge again, was met at the Horns Reef off Denmark by the 2nd Cruiser Squadron and the 7th Destroyer Flotilla, with the battlecruisers *Hood* and *Renown*. Also present was *Ark Royal* with the battleships *Rodney* and *Nelson*. This group of tempting targets, some 250 miles north-east of the German island of Heligoland, was shadowed by three Dornier 18 flying boats, circling just outside AA gun range.

Nine Skuas from 800 and 803 Squadrons took off, but at first had difficulty locating the Do 18s against the dark sea. 800's aircraft fired all their ammunition at one without noticeable result – the flying boat and one of its companions escaped. The third was attacked by a trio from 803 Squadron, one putting a bullet through the Dornier's radiator. Starved of coolant, the Dornier landed on the sea. A crewman waved his white overalls in surrender and all were picked up by the destroyer HMS *Somali*

The downed Dornier 18, shortly before it was sunk by gunfire. (After The Battle)

before the flying boat was sunk by gunfire. This was the first German aircraft destroyed by British forces in this war.

What happened next was an ominous pointer to the future. Any big ship was vulnerable to air attack and a Combat Air Patrol – a standing patrol of fighters overhead – not only gave advance warning but also some immediate defence if an attack was made. Despite this, Vice-Admiral Lionel Wells, flying his flag in *Ark Royal*, did not put up a CAP. All aircraft were struck down into the hangars, then drained of fuel to reduce the fire risk if the carrier was hit. This underlined the Navy's belief in AA fire as their primary defence – ignoring the fact that fighters, even Skuas, could intercept at a distance, breaking up an attack before it reached *Ark Royal*.

This stupidity nearly proved fatal. Within an hour – and undoubtedly summoned by the shadowing Dorniers – five Heinkel 111s appeared. Four were indeed driven off by AA fire, but the fifth made a determined attack, dropping a 1,000-kilo bomb. Her captain ordered a hard turn to starboard and the bomb exploded just off the port bow. *Ark Royal* rolled sideways, with water crashing over her flight deck and aircraft rolling loose below it. Then she righted herself.

Ju 88s of I/KG30 came next, diving out of cloud. *Hood* was hit on the port quarter, the bomb bouncing off to explode in the sea. Little damage was caused but Admiral Forbes, the Commander-in-Chief, was not impressed. Witnessing the attack from HMS *Nelson*, he criticised the battlecruisers' crews for a slow response to the threat.

Ark Royal's aircraft should have been up and actively patrolling. Not only did the Navy have inadequate aircraft, but it was apparent from this episode that not all senior officers knew how to use them properly. Despite this incident the lesson was not learned, resulting in the loss of HMS *Glorious* off Norway the following year.

The pilot claimed to have damaged *Ark Royal* and subsequent German air reconnaissance reported the two battleships but no carrier. Goebbels

The Junkers Ju 88, fastest of the Luftwaffe's bombers in 1939. (Author's collection)

inflated this and Hamburg radio broadcast the next day: 'We have an important announcement for listeners. Where is the *Ark Royal*? She was hit in a German attack on 26 September at 3 p.m. Where is the *Ark Royal*? Britons, ask your Admiralty.' The pilot, despite his protests, was decorated for his 'feat' and consequently became a laughing stock among his fellow officers.

A week later the *Völkischer Beobachter* showed an illustration of the carrier rearing out of the sea, with a massive explosion on her deck. On the 26th this paper had published a story claiming that Churchill had instructed the captain of a British submarine to torpedo the *Athenia*, hoping to bring America into the war. Churchill had to tell Roosevelt that this was untrue. In October he informed the War Cabinet that *Ark Royal* was with the Home Fleet and undamaged, but the Germans continued to broadcast the same claim, writing the carrier off more than once before she succumbed to a torpedo hit in the Mediterranean in 1941.

Young William Crawford, the bemused diarist aboard HMS *Belfast*, would now have something more interesting to write about. On 9 October the cruiser, while on the Northern Patrol, first intercepted a Norwegian ship, sending her to Kirkwall in the Orkneys for examination. Then what appeared to be a Swedish vessel came in sight, but sharp-eyed lookouts spotted that her original name had been replaced by another. *Belfast* signalled her to heave to or be fired on, then sent across a boarding party. Their suspicions were confirmed, for she was the *Cap Norte*, a German blockade runner. The prize money awarded to her crew was welcome.

Her First Officer, Erich Kappler, was furious. He had spent most of the previous war behind the wire, after being caught in much the same manner on another blockade runner twenty-five years before. Perhaps the matelots

Ark Royal under air attack – probably later in the war but indicating the dangers her crew had to face. (J&C McCutcheon Collection)

who marched him off into captivity again commented that he did not know how lucky he was.

During this month Churchill too had been lucky, though he did not know it at the time. On 30 October *Hood, Nelson* and *Rodney* covered an iron ore convoy from the Norwegian port of Narvik to Britain. North of the Orkneys *U-56* avoided ten escorting destroyers to fire three torpedoes at *Nelson*. Churchill, with Admirals Forbes and Pound, was aboard at the time. One missed, two failed to explode and nobody on board the battleship realised it then. All the U-boat's crew heard was the clang of metal on metal.

To Dönitz's frustration, the magnetic pistols fitted to German torpedoes at this time were often proving defective, possibly due to high sunspot activity affecting the earth's magnetism around this time – as the RAF discovered when their radio conversations became unintelligible during a magnetic storm.

The Royal Navy had had its losses, but its successes too, and no one could accuse it of being anything other than fully employed. Its next loss would be a massive one, in its own backyard.

3

THEY CALL THIS SPRING

They call this spring, Mum. They have one down here every year.
                    A child evacuee writing home from Kent, spring 1940

The first air raids on Britain had come in 1915, in East Anglia. Zeppelin airships, followed by Gotha and Gigant biplane bombers, then switched to London. A Zeppelin crew had carried out what was probably the first ever leaflet raid, dropping a piece of paper. Written in blue crayon, it said, 'You English. We have come and we will come again soon.' Which they did, up to May 1918, killing 1,413 civilians, 670 of them in London.

In 1924 the Home Office's Air Raid Precautions Committee met to look at the problem of future raids, with evacuation seen as a means of reducing casualties. Plans were drawn up to move government departments, industries and any civilians not vital to the war effort out of cities in the event of another war. Compulsion would be bad for morale; the population would have to be convinced of the need to move, then assisted to do so. With the assumption that better-off families would make their own arrangements, as in 1914–18, priority would go to poorer areas.

By the mid-1930s aviation's speedy advance and the Spanish Civil War showed that any future raids would not be confined to London. All centres of population would be in the firing line, as the experience of Guernica in 1937 showed. Hitler's Condor Legion had pounded this Basque town into rubble, killing 1,654 people and wounding 889.

Still the politicians debated. Evacuees would be split into three groups: those rich enough to help themselves; the aged, infirm, children and pregnant women; then civil servants and those who for commercial reasons needed to move into quieter areas. The best way to evacuate children was through their schools, softening the blow by allowing their friends to move with them, under teachers who were accustomed to giving instructions. Relaying these to the parents was easily done, either through the children themselves or by notes. The marshalling area would be the school itself, familiar to all.

The Munich Crisis of 1938 proved a useful rehearsal. Trenches were hastily dug in parks and gas masks were issued. Although an evacuation was started from London, panic was such that many had not waited, heading by train out to Wales or the West Country. The Divisional Food Officer for South Wales suddenly found himself saddled with 130,000 extra mouths. They would have been joined by half a million school children, but this move was cancelled at the last minute as Chamberlain flew home with his piece of paper.

All were home again by the end of October's first week, and for those in charge there were lessons to learn. Moving evacuees had been reasonably smooth, but all too often there had been no accommodation arranged at the other end, with people having to use village halls as dormitories.

As 1939 dawned fresh preparations were made, the government designating an area south of the Bristol Channel to the Wash for use by Londoners. In March schools were told how to reach their reception areas, and in May those who wished to be included in the scheme had to register. Mothers of under-fives could accompany their children and wherever possible families would be kept together.

On 24 August, as tension rose, the BBC broadcast to teachers in reception areas to report to their schools on the 26th, with a rehearsal two days later. Evacuation finally began on 1 September.

That Friday morning the school crocodiles formed up to head for their designated stations, to board 4,000 special trains. Mothers and relatives clustered round ticket barriers to bid a tearful goodbye, though at the last minute a few snatched their offspring back. Some travelled by bus, and would be on the road for up to two days. Others used pleasure steamers, but most would go by train, starting from city stations to turn onto sleepy rural branch lines.

Mothers and children waiting to be evacuated from London's Victoria station on Saturday 2 September. (IWM Neg. No. HU36237)

Doctor Brock, the headmistress of Mary Batchelor School in South London, witnessed a heartbreaking scene.

> One of the pictures I will always keep in my mind is our last view of the mothers and fathers waving through the railings above the station as we waved goodbye while the train steamed out of London. We had their children in trust, and to keep life as normal and safe and happy for them as possible was our task. As we went, the barrage balloons were slowly rising all around us – a strangely beautiful sight and a dramatic reminder of the reason for us going.

Despite the best attempts at organisation, with each school knowing which train it had to get onto, some groups turned up early and others late. Not surprisingly, they were then herded onto trains intended for others and plans began to go wrong. Anglesey, awaiting 625 children, received 2,468. Pwllheli, in North Wales, not expecting any, received 400. Other provincial towns, bracing themselves for an influx of thousands of city dwellers, often found themselves with less than half the numbers expected, even though over a million people were on the move.

This exodus was not confined to London's termini; coastal towns in the south-east were also seen as vulnerable. Southampton, Rochester, Chatham, Gillingham and Rainham decanted their children onto the Southern Railway's network, while the other companies took care of provincial cities, from Birmingham to Middlesbrough, Leeds and Glasgow.

Most children chattered excitedly, sticking to old friends while making new ones and looking on the journey as an adventure, while some smaller ones gazed moodily or tearfully out through the carriage windows, unable to understand why they were being sent away and what they had done to deserve it. Packed lunches, though meant for later in the day, were eaten as soon as they were out of sight of their families. Extra trains meant non-corridor stock, which led to boys relieving themselves out of a window, or a temporary stop somewhere amid the greenery. Then it was down the embankment to use the bushes.

In those days almost every village had its own station, often a clump of brick buildings amid the fields, some distance from the community it was meant to serve. It combined a tranquil atmosphere with short periods of intense activity by a few elderly staff, who in between trains spent much of their time gardening. Now, amid the cattle trucks and milk churns, came a grimy special, disgorging a pile of children with luggage labels tied to their lapels, proclaiming who they were and where they had come from. They lugged bags, pillowcases and treasured toys onto the platform, while harassed teachers tried to sort out who was to go where.

Those prevailed on to take them in eyed their charges with a mixture of curiosity and distaste. Older girls could help around the house, while their tall teenage brothers would be an asset in the fields, especially with younger farmhands now being called up into the Army. Often stations resembled a Roman slave market, with the better-dressed and cleaner arrivals promptly whisked away. The youngest and scruffiest remained until the billeting officer started mentioning compulsion.

It would be another fifty years before the term 'culture shock' was coined, but that was what awaited everyone. To a city child rural poverty came as a surprise, as did the discovery that milk originated, not from a clean United Dairies bottle, but from dirty cows that swished their tails in your face. Not only that, but apples grew on trees instead of magically appearing at the grocer's. A sow grunting in a muddy sty might put them off pork for a while, but the sight of spring lambs being born would be a source of awe and wonder.

Some easily adapted to this new life, welcoming the chance to run through meadows, climb over gates, come home muddy and learn the rudiments of poaching. Others took one look at the waving green acres, then promptly hitched a lift back to the city, in an age when it was still possible and (usually) safe to do so. Adolescents found, to their disgust, that provincial towns lacked any kind of nightlife. They would, however, eat well, and often more healthily, than they had before the war. Food was abundant in the countryside, in contrast to the rationing in towns.

Ignorance flourished in an age before television gave everyone some view of the world outside. The average East Ender's idea of a holiday had been a day trip to Southend or a week spent hop-picking on a Kent farm. For those who had known nothing but cobbled streets, dockland and squalid Victorian back-to-backs, the countryside was an alien world. It was green, it was strangely silent and it squelched when you trod in it. However, ignorance could cut both ways: the more intelligent arrivals commented among themselves on the narrow-mindedness around them, where anyone from the next town was looked on as an outsider.

Slum-dwellers saw thatched cottages with roses round the door, where going to bed meant climbing creaky old wooden stairs with a candle. Indeed, for some having a bed was unimaginable luxury, to say nothing of clean sheets and an inside toilet. Darkness, added to by the blackout, closed in and many a city child cowered under the blankets, afraid of the wind in the trees, the eerie midnight hooting of an owl or the bleating of sheep on the fells.

Others were less fortunate. Their new home could be an outlying farm, on the edge of a moorland hill, with mud around the back door, a front door they seldom used and tumbledown outbuildings knee-deep in nettles. Water would come from a hand pump in the yard and lighting either by gas or oil lamps. Their new 'mother' might be a kindly woman who had had children of her own, and was not surprised at the amount that boys ate, or a grey-haired hard-faced old crone in a long black dress who insisted on chapel attendance every Sunday, with silence strictly observed at mealtimes. Their stay might be for a week, or for over five years. Some of them would soon be on the move again, by ship to America, Canada or South Africa – and what a revelation that would be. Everything was strange, new and uncertain.

Some would stay for much longer. Pickering station, in Yorkshire's North Riding, welcomed a contingent of over 200 Middlesbrough Grammar School girls, resplendent in gabardine raincoats and velour hats. The city's steelworks and its coastal position had made it a prime target for bombing. One girl was taken in by the local Methodist minister's family, to become good friends with his son. In time the son was called up into the Royal Artillery, seeing action with 15th Scottish Division in the war's final year. He came home safely, they subsequently married, and at the time of the writing of this book they are still together.

Some evacuees never became happy away from home, and punishments could be extreme. Dennis Hayes, a seven-year-old evacuated from Portsmouth with his five-year-old brother to the village of Sway in Hampshire, was one. 'I can remember my brother crying most of the night, and so the father tied him to a banister at the foot of the stairs with a scarf. Of course, that made him cry even more.'

Other children were surprisingly stoic. Thirteen-year-old Elizabeth Mossman wrote to the *News Chronicle*:

> I'm sure it was a surprise for all us evacuees to find ourselves scattered about the country, taken to a new home and getting to know our new foster mothers and fathers. At first it was just like another holiday, but, after a time, a funny feeling of homesickness seemed to creep in, and I hoped and prayed that the war would end. But it was no use feeling downhearted, and if we evacuees do stay out of London, I'm sure we will be doing our bit for the country as well as helping the government.

The increased classes imposed on village schools led to some being conducted in the open air during the warm September weather, then in church halls, in stately homes, or using a system in which local children went to school in the morning, followed by the evacuees in the afternoon. An 'us and them' attitude led to gangs forming, with playground fights.

Locals often resented the newcomers on their patch, feeling that everything had been handed to them on a plate. The pub in the marketplace was full of tales of how little the 'vacees' knew about country life, or horror stories of impetigo and scabies. The newcomers, adjusting to expanding horizons, in turn tried to understand locals who wore flat caps, hitched up their trousers with hairy string and spoke with oo-arr voices. Those who stayed would begin to do the same as time went by.

Not all those on the move were children. In the first days of the war Southampton had witnessed a pin-striped panic as those who were well off, or who thought themselves too highly strung for war work, decamped to America on the first available liner, notwithstanding the *Athenia*'s fate.

Then there were middle-aged pompous women who headed for genteel boarding houses in the Lake District, remaining there for the duration, or at least until the gin ran out, while doing a little knitting for the boys overseas. One of them was well portrayed in the film *The Way to the Stars*, beginning every sentence with, 'As you know, I never complain, but...'

There was still no sign of the aerial apocalypse, and any aircraft heard overhead at night had been friendly. Despite government appeals, mothers came out to fetch their children home. They were not to know that within a year many of them would have to begin the process all over again.

*   *   *

For those left behind and those who returned during the first weeks of September, life for now seemed much as normal, with some added irritations. There was the gas mask, in its cardboard case, to be put on the hall table and remembered first thing in the morning, though it was not long before the handbag manufacturers came up with smarter, more durable containers.

Would gas be used again? By now there were middle-aged men with wheezy lungs, or an intermittent embarrassing skin itch, who had seen its effects in a trench while banging the empty shell case that had served as a warning gong. The Germans had been the first to use it, at Neuve Chapelle in 1915, swiftly followed by everyone else. The British Army had dubbed mustard gas shells 'Hun Stuff', then gone on to use them in the same fashion.

The soft plop when a gas shell landed nearby, the hiss of its contents, or an eerie silence as greenish-white clouds crept across no man's land behind advancing grotesque masked faces, like beings from another world – all these were unwelcome memories. There was also an attitude among senior officers that gas was a dirty, sneaky, underhand weapon – one that only 'they' would employ.

Gas shells had been stockpiled by both sides; the new 25-pounder field gun was capable of firing them. Gas mask chest packs would be carried by every British soldier in the field, and an anti-gas cape behind his head, tied in such a way that by pulling the string it would unroll down his back. Even in Egypt or the Malayan jungle such items were considered necessary. Service vehicles sported a blotch of sickly yellow paint on their bonnets, which would turn red if gas approached. On bomber airfields, well away from everything else, SCI dumps would be established. The designation 'Smoke Curtain Installation' was deliberately misleading. These bombs were lined with Bakelite and capable of being filled with a variety of toxic chemical agents.

To get children used to wearing their strange new rubber objects, and to make the younger ones think it was all a game, masks meant to look like Mickey Mouse were issued, with, for babies, a contraption resembling a latter-day space helmet. There was even a gas-proof dog kennel for the Canine Defence League. Some lessons would be conducted while wearing the masks, and those who did would remember how hot they became inside.

The Geneva Protocol of 1925 had banned the use of gas in time of war. It became British policy, upheld by all political parties, never to initiate the use of such weapons, though research continued at Porton Down in Wiltshire. These were not restricted to choking agents such as chlorine and phosgene, well known from the previous war. By the mid-1930s German chemists had developed tabun, sarin and soman – all of them colourless and odourless. One poster featured a gas mask, with the phrase 'Hitler Will Send No Warning'. It was not yet known that, having himself been temporarily blinded by mustard gas in 1918, he was reluctant to use it again.

For now, there was the blackout to see to in the evening, with the use of heavy dark curtains. Factories resorted to painting their windows and skylights black, with ventilation often going by the board. The shout of 'Put that light out!' echoed down Acacia Avenue, and its originator, the local air-raid warden, with his armband and tin hat, became the most hated figure in Britain. Muttered comparisons with Hitler were made, with allegations that the said warden's parents had met only once, and anyone rash enough to light a cigarette in a darkened street could find himself in court explaining why. A German pilot a mile up might have seen it. Everyone knew that.

The blackout brought other dangers, with road accidents increasing at an alarming rate. Some people stopped going out altogether when darkness came, while casualty departments lost count of those who fell down steps, into canals, through plate-glass windows or walked into telegraph poles. By the end of 1939 it was estimated that one fifth of the population had suffered some blackout-related accident. Tree trunks and lamp standards received white stripes, while platform and pavement edges were whitened as a precaution. Torches became essential, but anyone careless enough to point one skywards might be accused of signalling to the enemy. A dance band tune of the time was 'Crash, Bang, I Wanna Go Home'.

Rail travel became an ordeal. Trains were late, dirty and often cancelled. When they did arrive they were usually crammed full of Forces personnel and their kitbags, all trying to go somewhere. Ticket prices rose in an attempt to put the public off travelling, and posters on railway stations read 'Is Your Journey Really Necessary?'

The bulbs in carriages were now a dull blue, limiting the light they gave. Most services were still steam-hauled and the smoke could not be disguised, but a tarpaulin over the cab now covered the glow from the firebox door. The carriage windows were similarly protected, and passengers pulling the curtains aside defied a cautionary notice, which read, 'That fabric on the window is for your protection.' It was not long before witty graffiti artists amended 'window' to 'widow'.

Curving steps highlighted by white-painted dashes – just one of many blackout hazards.
(IWM Neg. No. HU101916)

Not content with this, officialdom invented a nattily attired cartoon character,
Mister Billy Brown of London Town, who self-righteously declared:

I trust you'll pardon my correction,
That stuff is there for your protection.

To which exasperated passengers were wont to write:

We thank you for your information
We want to see the bloody station.

The situation would become even worse in the middle of 1940, when the
invasion threat led to all station signs being removed, but that was yet to
come.

The 1930s had been something of a golden era for the railways, with heavy
demand in the summer months for travel to seaside resorts. Scarborough, on
Yorkshire's east coast, was one of the busiest. In 1939 my grandmother,
then running a four-storey guesthouse on Blenheim Terrace, overlooking the
town's North Bay, quickly saw her fortunes change. The rest of the houses in
this road were similar and, in common with many resorts, were requisitioned
by the Army, while barbed wire appeared on the rocky beach below.

It had been a time when up to twenty guests were fed three times a day, staying from Saturday to Saturday. With two young children and a baby as well, my grandmother's kitchen was seldom quiet, but hard work was part of her life and anything was better than the poverty she and my grandfather had left behind in Sheffield. He had converted a large pantry in the basement into an air-raid shelter. My mother, nine when the war broke out and herself almost evacuated to Canada, later remembered a string of incidents during the first months:

> The Army wanted to requisition her house as well, but she got round it for a long while by taking in officers' wives. Next door was the sergeants' mess, with a cook called Ginger. One day there was a commotion, with soldiers lining up in the road outside. When she asked Ginger what was happening, he told her 'Hitler's invaded'. So we all ended up in the shelter with our gas masks on. After a while nothing had happened, so we all came up and everything was going on as normal. Ginger said 'I was only joking', and she hit him!

On 10 November the war came a little nearer when a Dornier 18 flying boat was brought down into the sea two miles off Scarborough by a pair of Lockheed Hudsons from 220 Squadron. One man was lost and the others rescued by Dutch ships. Then there was the day when a German aircraft shot up a small, unarmed fishing boat that was making its way back to the harbour. The crew tried to get close in to the cliffs by the castle to avoid the attacks, while all the family could do was watch. Tears streamed down my grandmother's face – the first time, my mother said, that she had ever seen her display any emotion. Soldiers ran out into the road with rifles, but any firing would have been a waste of ammunition. My grandfather was so irate he would have used one anyway. The boat limped into the harbour and was later seen out of the water with a severely damaged wheelhouse. It was the kind of incident that brought home the fact that, yes, there really was a war.

Scarborough would not be severely raided until 1941, but aircraft prowled by night, and at Blenheim Terrace the family cat developed an ability to tell the difference between 'ours' and 'theirs', by the engine noise. If it stayed outside, nothing would happen. If it came running in, 'they' were overhead.

At homes around the country, those who had back gardens dug a 4-foot-deep hole in them to accommodate the Anderson shelter, named after the current Home Secretary. Sold to those who could afford it, it was also freely available to those families on less than £250 a year. It was a two-man job to bolt together the large corrugated sections it consisted of, while commenting to the neighbours that it looked like Meccano for adults. Despite a flimsy appearance, it was capable of withstanding a miss at 25 yards from a 1,000-kilo bomb, the earth heaped on top providing further resistance to blast. However, leaks occurred in some areas where the water table was just below the surface, and the four bunks inside proved too short for taller people to sleep in comfortably. Nobody yet knew that aluminium powder added to German explosive doubled its power. Nobody, that was, except the British Treasury, which had vetoed this refinement for the RAF on the grounds of cost.

Tape was used to criss-cross windows, to lessen the risk of flying glass, and cigarette cards showed how to put out an incendiary bomb. Using more tape and sheets, one room within a house could be made gas-proof. Older people, with memories of 'the Zepps', opted to shelter beneath the stairs, which would often turn out to be the safest place. For anyone afflicted by life's troubles – not necessarily war-related ones – the place to go was the Citizens' Advice Bureau, which had been established on 4 September as a wartime emergency measure.

So, having made your contribution to today's war effort and arrived home safely by whatever means, what else was there to do? Fear of raids had resulted in cinemas, theatres and other places of entertainment closing at the beginning of the war, but the continuing quiet soon saw them opened again.

For many 'the wireless' was the primary diversion, although a glut of programmes featuring Sandy Macpherson, the BBC theatre organist since

Delivering Anderson shelter parts to a London & North Eastern Railway goods yard. (IWM Neg. No. HU101690)

Taping household windows as a precaution against bomb blast. (IWM Neg. No. HU102255)

1938, led to various suggestions as to what he could do with his organ! News bulletins came on the hour, the one at nine in the evening being the most important. The comedian Tommy Handley on *ITMA* (*It's That Man Again*) summed up the nation's feelings with his Office of Twerps, at the Ministry of Aggravation and Mysteries. His programme was listened to across Europe, often by people who never understood it, simply because it contained the sound of laughter.

Music has always tended to travel one way across the Atlantic – a process only temporarily reversed by the Beatles in the mid-1960s. Some American songs at the war's outbreak seemed by their tone to either anticipate the hardships to come, or to symbolise bereavement. There was 'Rendezvous Time in Paris' by Louise Tobin, then the wife of jazz trumpeter Harry James, and Dick Powell's 'I Get Along Without You Very Well'. Those wishing for a better future could sigh over 'When You Wish upon a Star' by Cliff Evans, the voice of Jiminy Cricket in Walt Disney's *Pinocchio*, accompanied by the usual saccharin-voiced choir.

A singer later to be termed 'The voice of the twentieth century' was about to reach a wider audience. Harry James had heard Frank Sinatra in a New Jersey radio show. Knowing his was the voice he wanted for the ballads of the day, James had phoned the studio and signed Sinatra for the next seven months, recording 'On a Little Street in Singapore' with him during October 1939.

Other transatlantic offerings seemed to encourage an escape from present troubles. In the western *Destry Rides Again* Marlene Dietrich sang 'See What the Boys in the Back Room Will Have' as she became involved with James Stewart on and off screen, while Bing Crosby crooned his way through 'An Apple for the Teacher' with Connie Boswell.

The war would see a change in the fortunes of many of Britain's own entertainers. Vera Lynn, then twenty-two, had been at home with her family and the saxophonist Harry Lewis, whom she would marry two years later, when war broke out. Her first engagement had been in a working-men's club at the age of seven. At sixteen she had begun singing with dance bands, and wondered now if the war would put an end to her career. Instead, it was to take off and she would personify the girl next door, patiently waiting for her man to return. Her March 1940 hit 'Who's Taking You Home Tonight?' was accompanied by an early synthesiser, and her live radio programme *Sincerely Yours*, which began in 1941, ran on and off for the next four years.

The products of the British music hall added their talents. Bud Flanagan and Chesney Allen sang 'Run, Rabbit, Run' which, depending on what you wanted to believe, was either a slighting reference to Hitler, or to the rabbit allegedly killed in the first raid on the Orkneys, of which more in Chapter 4. Another item in their repertoire was 'We're Gonna Hang out the Washing on the Siegfried Line':

We're gonna hang out the washing on the Siegfried Line
Have you any dirty washing, mother dear?
We're gonna hang out the washing on the Siegfried Line
'Cause the washing day is here.
Whether the weather may be wet or fine
We'll just rub along without a care.
We're gonna hang out the washing on the Siegfried Line
If the Siegfried Line's still there!

This song had been inspired by a *Daily Express* cartoon, in which a soldier writing home had used the phrase. The Germans were offended, ascribing this song to 'the Jewish scribes of the BBC'. Eventually the washing would indeed be hung out as described, but only when the British 21st Army Group finally moved forward into Germany five years later.

Anyone turning the wireless knob after the BBC's nine o'clock news would hear voices of a very different kind, relayed by the then-neutral Radio Luxembourg. English was spoken, but not by someone friendly to them.

'This is Station Bremen and Station Hamburg, on the 30-metre band.'

There was a drawling Oxbridge tone, accentuated by the microphone.

'Jairmany calling, Jairmany calling.'

William Joyce, of Irish-American origin, had been a member of Sir Oswald Mosley's British Union of Fascists before falling out with his leader and setting up his own National Socialist League. Rightly suspecting that anyone deemed sympathetic to Nazism would shortly be interned, he and his wife had fled to Germany in August 1939. He had found employment, first as a newsreader, then as a broadcaster of propaganda. Although often laughably wide of the mark, there were times when he came uncomfortably close to it. A reporter described him as an aristocrat of the 'dammit-get-out-of-my-way' type, and his distinctive voice caused the British public to dub him 'Lord Haw-Haw'.

'We know about that clock in Banstead. It is slow even today.'

Inevitably, there was a credulous minority who believed him. If he knew this, might he not have access to British military secrets? The good citizens of Banstead, in Surrey, checked their clock and found it to be correct. Following a slogan of the day, they kept calm and carried on.

Joyce's new masters were evidently pleased, for at Christmas 1939 he received a box of cigars from Goebbels, then an even bigger one from Göring. Propaganda is that branch of lying which consists in nearly deceiving your friends, without quite deceiving your enemies.

Those fond of more cultured live entertainment had the Royal Ballet, then only ten years old. Based at Sadler's Wells in North London, it owed its existence to Dame Ninette de Valois, the renowned dancer and choreographer. The company spent ten weeks boosting morale in London, then a further ten around the country. A tour of France, Belgium and Holland would bring them too close to the action in May 1940, necessitating an escape by cargo boat when the Germans invaded. Their dancers included the young Margot Fonteyn.

For those who preferred classical music without the spectacle of men in tights, there was Dame Myra Hess, the noted concert pianist. On the war's outbreak she had locked both her Steinway pianos, declaring she would not play again until peace returned. However, it was not long before she changed her mind. The National Gallery's Director, Kenneth Clark, had anticipated future events by evacuating most of its paintings to a slate quarry in Wales. The empty dome hall proved an ideal platform for a series of lunchtime concerts given by her. These proved surprisingly popular, a famous film sequence shot by documentary maker Humphrey Jennings showing the Queen among the audience.

If you wanted to dance – and who could resist the latest craze, the Lambeth Walk? – then London's West End offered plenty of choice, with more bands now than before the war. There were plenty of customers, with formal evening dress no longer being the rule, except at the Café de Paris. Here the West Indian bandleader Ken 'Snakehips' Johnson had a residency. His friend, the top British vocalist Al Bowlly, often sang there. It was billed as 'the safest restaurant in London'.

The war's effects came a little closer when petrol rationing was introduced on 16 September. Most cars went into garages, on blocks for the duration, often with their tyres removed to recycle the rubber, or were commandeered by the Forces. For their owners, it meant a return to work by bus, train or tram for the next five years. Cars now became the preserve of those with a particular reason for using them, such as doctors, country vets or high-ranking civil servants, who could claim an extra allocation of fuel. Every drop was precious and, in an era before North Sea oil, it would have to be brought from the Caribbean in the Merchant Navy's tankers.

None of this prevented the underworld from taking advantage. Black market petrol was stored in garages, sheds, cellars or even buried in back gardens. Other goods changed hands, aided by the blackout. The NAAFI – caterers to the Forces – lost several million pounds in cigarette raids, while vehicles ferried over to France frequently arrived without spares or parts, adding to existing equipment shortages. Some British soldiers, knowing that French troops were using leave to make a little on the side, decided to do the same.

Service crime across the Channel became so serious that the War Office sent over 500 staff with police experience to deal with it, while at home desertion became a fact of life. From 1940 ration books became essential for deserters, changing hands at £2 a time. The blackout aided smash-and-grab raiders. A raid on Ciro's Pearls in Bond Street cleaned it out, and proved to be the first of several during the 1939/40 winter. The 'spiv', that dubious oily-haired character in the camelhair coat on the street corner, seemed to have access to anything, including those new nylon stockings that had first gone on sale in New York in the autumn of 1939.

After some government dithering, and accusations of profiteering, on 8 January 1940 food rationing was introduced. Supermarkets had yet to come to Britain and this was the age of the corner shop, at which you had to register.

The first foods to go on ration were butter, at 4 ounces per person per week, sugar (12 ounces), then bacon and ham (4 ounces). Other meat was rationed to the value of 1s 10d (9p) per person per week, so many housewives bought a large amount of a cheap cut for stewing or braising. Cheese, jam and tea followed, though fish, fruit, offal and vegetables were not rationed. Priority was given to children, and eggs became scarcer, often being replaced by the infamous dried egg powder. Oranges disappeared altogether, and the song 'Yes, We Have No Bananas' took on a new significance. Chalked signs indicating shortages appeared outside the local grocer's, queues formed, coupons were exchanged and housewives walked away with their allocation. As always, the black market meant that certain items were kept under the counter for the favoured few.

Speaking of food, anyone exercising their dog on the local common might find they were the only ones doing so. A fear of shortages and disruption from bombing led to the destruction of over 2 million pets. A booklet had advised on how to do this humanely and it was not confined to domestic animals. Regent's Park Zoo closed for the first time in its 110-year history. To the regret of their keepers, the poisonous snakes and Black Widow spiders were destroyed on 1 September, in case an exploding bomb allowed them to escape. Constricting snakes survived, as they could do little harm even if they got out. The aquarium was emptied of 200,000 gallons of water, being used to store newsprint and paper, while the keepers now carried rifles to shoot any large escaping carnivore. Twelve other animals, including the riding elephants, were evacuated to Whipsnade Zoo.

There would be other enemies later, but for now Italy and Japan were remaining neutral. Not that that surprised a lot of people. The strutting Mussolini had seemed a joke from the start – though the Ethiopians would not have agreed – and for all his hot air evidently lacked the guts to take on a country his own size. Japan, fully occupied in China, posed no immediate threat to Britain or her colonies. Anyway, the Japanese had no sense of balance through being carried on their mothers' backs as children, their eyesight was poor, their aircraft were outdated and they were unable to fly in the dark. Everyone knew that.

Then there was Ireland, most of it independent since 1922, but with six of Ulster's nine counties still under British control. The IRA, whose motto was 'England's difficulty is Ireland's opportunity', had recently mounted a bombing campaign in mainland Britain, gloatingly reported in the German press. It had culminated in the Coventry bicycle bomb murder on 25 August 1939, killing five people and injuring sixty others in that city's Broadgate shopping centre.

Eamon de Valera, Ireland's Taoiseach (President) and himself a veteran of the struggle for independence, was not taking sides. His declaration of neutrality made the country a possible back door for German agents to enter Britain, although those caught by the Garda would remain securely locked up for the duration. Arms, explosives and radios were sent by the Germans in the hope of attacking British military installations in the north.

Little was achieved, for the IRA turned out to be exasperatingly amateur, rejecting outside advice. During January 1940 they blew up the Royal Ordnance arms factory at Waltham Abbey in Essex, killing five people and injuring thirty. Once Churchill became Prime Minister the following May, he made it clear to de Valera that he would not tolerate Ireland being used as a terrorist base. If the Irish government did not crack down, he would. The IRA was riven with leadership struggles, some thinking de Valera a traitor, and most Irishmen hated the Germans for attacking Catholic Poland. Although it did send condolences on Hitler's death in 1945, the Irish government distanced itself from the IRA, whose activities faded.

The German Embassy would remain in Dublin throughout the war – referred to in Ireland as 'The Emergency' – and continued to send back weather reports. Ireland was now becoming a safe haven for deserters, some of whom would appear as extras alongside Laurence Olivier in the film *Henry V*.

Conscription was not enforced in Northern Ireland, which led to over 35,000 Ulstermen crossing the Irish Sea to join up at Liverpool. A similar number of Irish men and women did the same. Commendable though this was, what was more important, especially from the Royal Navy's point of view, was that the bases they had used on Ireland's west coast had been given up before the war and were no longer available to them, to Churchill's fury. There were mutterings about U-boat crews using Ireland's isolated west coast, but nothing was ever proven.

Finally, how stood the Empire? Appeasement had in part been based on uncertainty about whether the self-governing Dominions would support Britain. On 3 September Australia immediately joined in. Before very long the RAAF's 10 Squadron, equipped with Sunderlands, would serve with Coastal Command. New Zealand promptly cabled support, and on the 10th Canada declared war. India's Viceroy, Lord Linlithgow, committed the subcontinent to war without consulting any of the native politicians.

South Africa, with the Boer War's legacy of bitterness, had, after a stormy debate, declared war on the 6th, the decision being taken by a majority of the white minority. However, those who had opposed their country's intervention did not give up. In January 1940 Jan Hertzog, the former Prime Minister, joined with the Nationalist Party to pass a motion calling for an end to South Africa's involvement. It was defeated by twelve votes in the House of Assembly. An Afrikaner resistance movement known as the *Ossewa Brandwag* – the 'Wagon Burners' – formed, one of whose members was John Vorster, a future Prime Minister at the height of the apartheid era. It was a fine land whose sunny climate would give some evacuees sanctuary until 1945, and RAF trainee pilots useful flying practice, but they would face hostility from some civilians.

What would happen next? Wherever the action was, it seemed not to be here. The skies remained quiet, at least by day, the wardens played cards in their posts and the recently recruited Auxiliary Fire Service took out its taxi cabs with their trailer pumps to rescue cats from trees. Journalists, hard put to find any heroic stories, competed for snappy titles. These included the Bore War, the Sitzkreig, the Drole de Guerre and of course the Phoney War – coined by an American reporter.

It all seemed easy and undemanding, unless you were at sea or living in central Europe. Princess Margaret summed up the feelings of many people. 'Who is this Hitler, spoiling everything?'

4

DESTINATION ORKNEY

This bloody town's a bloody cuss
No bloody trams, no bloody bus
No one cares for bloody us
In bloody Orkney.

Soldiers' poem

In the autumn of 1939 it would have seemed to most people that the Orkney Islands, off the north-east coast of Scotland, were the remotest of places, in an area far removed from European events, and the last place anyone would expect to confront an enemy. It was a quiet area, with fishing and farming the main occupations. The only major settlements were the towns of Kirkwall and Stromness. However, Scapa Flow, an anchorage surrounded by islands, might have been designed for such an eventuality.

In the eighth century the Vikings colonised the Orkneys – perhaps a reason why Orcadians tend not to think of themselves as Scots – and Norse words found their way into the local language. Scapa comes from *skalpr*, meaning longboat, and *skalpei*, meaning an isthmus that boats could have been hauled over – probably a reference to the flat land between Scapa Flow and Kirkwall Bay. Flow comes from *flot*, meaning a large body of water.

Some 10 miles across in each direction, the Flow is bordered by the islands of Hoy to the west, with South Walls, Fara and Flotta to the south. South Ronaldsay lies to the east, as part of a string of small islands, while to the north and north-east are the shores of what Orcadians call the Mainland. The Flow's depth of up to 30 fathoms can accommodate the largest vessels, while the ring of land gives shelter from the worst storms. The main entrance, then used by capital ships, is Hoxa Sound, between Flotta and South Ronaldsay. Destroyers and smaller vessels used Switha Sound, to the west.

Until the early years of the twentieth century, much of the Royal Navy's fleet in home waters had been concentrated in the south, with France, as the traditional enemy, in mind. The Anglo-German arms race had made it clear that in the event of future hostilities the North Sea would be important too, leading Rosyth and Cromarty, in north-eastern Scotland, to become naval bases. In 1909 the Home and Atlantic Fleets visited the Flow, beginning an association with it that would last for almost half a century.

The Flow's advantages were clear. It was large enough to hold the Grand Fleet, its remote location made spying more difficult and submarine attack was considered 'practically impossible', although by 1912 this attitude was beginning to change, with an attack by fast torpedo-carrying destroyers now also becoming a threat. Royal Marines and locally recruited Territorial Army members provided the defences.

During 1914–18 the Flow became an important base, but under the threat of the mine and torpedo. Admiral Sir John Jellicoe, who commanded the Grand Fleet from the war's outbreak, later said that he had never worried about his ships while they were on the move at sea, but only when they lay at anchor. Rear Admiral H. W. Grant, then the skipper of the ill-fated cruiser HMS *Hampshire*, said after the war:

> We spent one winter in Scapa Flow and the whole time were under steam. At that time Scapa Flow was not a healthy place to live in, because we were never sure whether the Hun would get a submarine in. We had a good many scares and had to raise steam. Week after week we were constantly going in and out of Scapa Flow by night.

Lookout and searchlight posts appeared on the islands, with old expendable ships being sunk to block some of the narrow eastern channels between them. A minefield was laid off Hoy Sound, while hydrophone systems, backed up by newly invented depth charges, listened for engine sounds beneath the water. Losses around the islands included Lord Kitchener, who went missing when HMS *Hampshire* was mined in 1916.

After the war's end, on 21 June 1919, the Flow witnessed an extraordinary spectacle. The German High Seas Fleet, brought over there after the Armistice, scuttled itself rather than hand its ships over to their former enemies. Rear Admiral von Reuter, who had been in charge, was given a dressing down before departing with his men for home. An epic salvage operation by the firm of Cox & Danks followed in the interwar years and some astonishing film was shot of huge ships rising, weed-covered, to the surface. The hulks were towed away for scrapping at Rosyth. By 1939 the battlecruiser *Derfflinger*, which had proved a stubborn case, lay bottom-up off the island of Rysa, where she would remain for the duration of the war. Seven vessels were too deep to be salvaged, although some scrap was brought up from them.

In 1938 improvements to the Flow's defences began, with the laying of anti-submarine booms. In August 1939 Hatston airfield, known as HMS *Sparrowhawk*, became operational. Lyness, which had housed the Navy's headquarters since 1919, now had accommodation for eighty-five staff – not a good situation, as 1,200 could be expected if war came. As it would be the main refuelling point, tunnels and storage tanks were built there, although this work would not be completed until 1943. Commander O. M. Frewin, the Senior Naval Officer and Harbourmaster, set up shop in the Kirkwall Hotel, but suffered from a lack of funds. At first he had no boat, having to borrow an RAF launch, and his request for a new quay at Lyness was turned down on the grounds of cost. He had to make do with an existing rotten structure until a drifter demolished it in 1941.

His Army opposite number, Brigadier Geoffrey Kemp MC, was no better off. On 29 September he arrived to lead the Orkney and Shetland Defences, but found little to command. Setting up his headquarters in Kirkwall's Stromness Hotel – he would have preferred the Kirkwall Hotel but the Navy had got there first – his troops consisted of eight heavy anti-aircraft guns at Lyness, five guns at a coastal battery and three Bren light machine guns to defend the newly installed RAF radar site at Netherbutton. There was one company of Seaforth Highlanders and another of Royal Engineers – just 500 men to defend the Fleet and police the coastline. He too had to borrow a civilian boat in order to get around.

On a good day, the islands have a certain stark beauty, with a light described as magical, green fields and treeless heather-clad moorland. Any off-duty birdwatchers would have found themselves in paradise. The bleak winters were a different story. In December the sun rises at nine in the morning, setting at three. The Orcadians claim that 'If you survive three winters, you'll stay here.' For many sailors, soldiers and airmen, one was enough. A posting to Scapa Flow was hated, and the leave train heading north to Thurso was full of gloomy faces, not helped by a sea crossing of the notoriously violent Pentland Firth. Some First World War veterans had actually preferred the Western Front's trenches to going through all that again.

Such northern latitudes led to extreme weather conditions. In summer a book could be read outside at midnight and in winter there was that strange phenomenon, the Aurora Borealis or Northern Lights. Light emitted from the upper atmosphere over the polar regions resembled that of an electrical discharge. Although sometimes dark red, it usually appeared as an eerie waving green curtain in the sky.

On duty there was often little else to do except shiver inside a duffel coat while staring from a cliff top at the sea. At the war's beginning accommodation consisted of huts and mud. The bar, if there was one, was usually in another hut, consisting of a trestle table and a few barrels. Soldiers who had never been to the Klondike speculated that it must have been like this. For the most far-flung units, the weekly arrival of the ration truck seemed like a major event.

Sports were laid on in an effort to keep fit and raise morale. Those stationed close to Kirkwall and Stromness were a bit better off. A good meal was available from the Lyness NAAFI, followed by a film, though usually an old one, either there or at the Junction Cinema in Kirkwall. ENSA concerts, with acts ranging from comedian George Formby to the classical violinist Yehudi Menuhin, were appreciated, not least because they showed that the Orkney garrison had not been entirely forgotten by the outside world.

Farming on Orkney had been depressed between the wars, but was now boosted by the demands of up to 60,000 men and women. Even at low wartime prices mortgages could be paid off and profits made. After 1945 it would become a land of owner-farmers, although they would probably have felt like locking up their daughters whenever the Home Fleet sailed in. Anyone seeking female company often went without. One Wren who was posted there commented, 'There are six hundred men to every girl, and I'm going to enjoy myself!'

HMS *Iron Duke*, Jellicoe's flagship at Jutland, was used for administration and as a detention centre. Two of her turrets were removed although, curiously, the ammunition in the magazines beneath remained. By the end of August 1939 there were forty-four ships in the Flow, including the recently commissioned aircraft carrier *Ark Royal*. On 1 September Admiral Sir Charles Forbes took them to sea, partly as a precaution but also to escort convoys, while supporting the Northern Patrol. Ships intercepted during this duty would be checked over at Kirkwall – a thankless but necessary task.

This time any future threat would not be confined to the sea, especially as the RAF estimated the Luftwaffe could drop 450 tons of bombs on the anchorage in a day. From 1938 the TA expanded again, recruiting men for a local unit. The Admiralty preferred to have its bases defended by the Royal Marines – a bone of contention during 1914–18 that flared up again now. The Orcadian soldiers were unhappy at the prospect of serving under Marine officers, and it was not until the middle of 1940 that the matter was resolved, with control of anti-aircraft units passing to the Army. As elsewhere, the matter was bedevilled by an initial lack of guns, equipment and radar facilities.

Long-serving sailors recalled the fate of *U-116*, which in October 1918 had tried to sneak into the Flow beneath a British warship passing though Hoxa Sound. It had been detected by a hydrophone station and destroyed by a shore-controlled mine – the last U-boat casualty of the First World War and the only one lost in such a manner. Now, once again, apart from minefields, indicator and guard loops lay across the approaches at Hoy and Hoxa Sound. A pre-war boom test with the battleship *Resolution* had resulted in her being stopped from a speed of 7 knots. Anti-submarine netting hung in the water like latter-day chainmail.

Then there was the question of the blockships. Those sunk in the last war were still in place, but there were still gaps between the islands on the eastern side of the anchorage that allowed smaller vessels to pass through. Or perhaps a surfaced submarine. Admiral Forbes had personally inspected them in June 1939, declaring them to be still navigable, despite the Admiralty's claims. Consequently, twenty more blockships were purchased, although the Treasury, penny-pinching as always, placed a cost limit of £10,000 on each one. During the first two months of the war they began to arrive.

On 15 September Churchill inspected the defences, being assured that they were as good as in the last war, with improvements now being added. Though pleased that his beloved Navy's discipline and ceremonial routine remained unchanged, he was aware that many of the senior officers he had once known were now either dead or retired, leaving him feeling like a relic from another age. The uniforms were the same, but the faces above them were younger. He could not help noting that many of the ships were old. Despite the misgivings this gave him, he felt that Britain still ruled the waves and returned to London. Admiral Sir Dudley Pound greeted him with news of the sinking of HMS *Courageous*. Churchill replied, 'We can't expect to carry on a war like this without that sort of thing happening from time to time. I have seen lots of it before.'

*   *   *

So far, German activity over the Flow had confined itself to aerial reconnaissance, the first being on 6 September. Lyness had been photographed on the 26th. There had been no raids yet, but nevertheless the Home Fleet sailed on 13 October, leaving a few older vessels behind. These included the elderly aircraft carrier *Pegasus*, the armed merchant cruiser *Rawalpindi* and the Royal Sovereign-class battleship *Royal Oak*.

Commissioned in 1916, *Royal Oak* had seen action at Jutland, claiming two hits. Her next meeting with the High Seas Fleet had been escorting it into the Flow. More recently she had seen active service in the Mediterranean on one of the neutrality patrols intended to deter weapons from reaching Franco's insurgents during the Spanish Civil War. Over an eighth of a mile long, displacing 29,150 tons, her hull was protected by a 13-inch armoured belt from her main deck to 5 feet beneath her waterline. Additional protection came in the form of two huge torpedo blisters, one either side. Her eight 15-inch guns could shell targets 13 miles away.

Formidable as this sounded, by 1939 she was old and incapable of keeping up with the main body of the Fleet. She had therefore been left behind as a floating anti-aircraft platform, in the eastern part of the anchorage, well away from Lyness, to protect Kirkwall and the nearby Netherbutton radar site. Conforming to blackout regulations, her riding lights had been painted blue, making them visible from only a short distance, and her porthole glasses had been replaced by plywood ventilators, which kept light in, but were not waterproof. As she was in harbour, to allow work to go on, not all of her watertight doors were closed. The nearest ship to her was *Pegasus*, 2 miles away.

Aboard was Surgeon-Lieutenant Dick Caldwell, who had been on her when the war began. That night the toast in the officers' wardroom had been 'Damnation to Hitler!' This evening he had played poker and listened to records with two other officers. He was not to know that he would never see them again.

HMS *Royal Oak*. The recognition stripes on B turret indicate that this shot was taken during the Spanish Civil War. (IWM)

Royal Oak had recently returned from a gruelling patrol between the Orkneys and Shetlands, while other ships had sailed further out after a report that the battlecruiser *Gneisenau* was off Norway. A tremendous gale had damaged her Carley floats and flooded the battery deck. She had been ordered back to the Flow, arriving on the 11th. The next day a German aircraft flew over, photographing her and the nearby battlecruiser *Repulse*.

It has been said that *Royal Oak* was not a happy ship and that the officers treated the men like cattle. Whatever their relations, the storm they had recently returned from had helped to build up that sense of shared ordeal that binds a crew together. After clearing up the shambles and taking on further stores, those released from duty had been able on the 13th to don their best uniforms and take the liberty boat, the drifter *Daisy II*, to sample the delights of Kirkwall. Some of them would board her again that night in very different circumstances.

The war still seemed a long way away. Apart from the blackout and a change of their hat tallies to read 'HMS' – the ship's name being deleted for security reasons – for the average matelot it seemed to be business as usual.

Jack Wood, an eighteen-year-old sailor from Langley Park in County Durham, had found time to write home. Referring to a family budgerigar, his letter read:

> The bird will keep you all company and will amuse me when I come home, though this is not very certain. Don't worry about me, because I am OK. You would not think there was a war where I am; everything is so quiet.

As for Churchill, for a few aboard *Royal Oak* it was a reminder of other similar times. Commander R. F. Nichols, the battleship's senior executive officer, had been a young midshipman on HMS *Vanguard* in July 1917, with *Royal Oak*, then a new ship, alongside her in the Flow. Suddenly *Vanguard* had suffered a magazine explosion, blowing her to pieces. Few had survived from those on board. Nichols had avoided this by attending a show staged by *Royal Oak*'s sailors on the theatre ship *Gourko*. The show had lasted longer than intended, causing him to miss his liberty boat back to the doomed ship. He had, therefore, lived on for another twenty-two years. What would the others have said had they seen him wearing three rings? Now here he was, aboard a ship that could also have been lost that night, back in an anchorage full of memories.

German naval analysts, perhaps as a result of aerial photographs, had realised that Kirk Sound, on the east side of the Flow, was not completely blocked off. During the First World War it had been, but afterwards, in response to requests from local fishermen, one ship had been removed and a second, the *Numidian*, swung round to open up a 200-yard gap between her and another ship, the *Thames*. This meant that by 1939 there was one ship in the middle of the Channel, one sunken one in its deepest part and one almost parallel to the Mainland shore.

The Admiralty had realised this deficiency, and early in 1939 another ship, the *Seriano*, had been sunk, partially filling the gap, the distance between herself and the *Thames* being partly blocked by hawsers. On the afternoon of 13 October another blockship, the *Lake Neuchatel*, had arrived, but had yet to be sunk in position.

Passing through all this meant a difficult dogleg, but it was an opportunity not to be missed. Submariners are a peculiar breed and their captains, whatever their navy, tended to be young, ambitious, driven men, capable of operating on their own. Unlike on a surface ship, anyone who tried hard enough could achieve a command while under thirty. Such a man was Kapitänleutnant Günther Prien, who had already sunk three steamers that September. His command, *U-47*, had sailed from Kiel on 8 October, maintaining radio silence. He now lay submerged off the eastern shores of the Orkneys, waiting for darkness.

Dönitz, recalling his own time underwater, had no doubt recognised the personal qualities needed for an attack of this kind. The grudge he had borne against the Royal Navy for over twenty years would now at last be paid off – and where better than Scapa Flow, the graveyard of the High Seas Fleet?

Late on the evening of the 13th, *U-47* surfaced. Prien headed for Skerry Sound, then realised his mistake and turned for Kirk Sound, to pass between the island of Lamb Holm and the Mainland. As he drew nearer to them, the three blockships became visible, the *Thames* being to port, the *Seriano* ahead and the *Numidian* to starboard. Prien identified two gaps and selected the northern one, between the *Seriano* and *Numidian*. By now he was behind time, although the tide was running with him into the Flow. He passed only 15 metres from the *Numidian*, entering the 60-metre-wide channel between the Mainland and north of the *Seriano*.

Suddenly Prien saw an anchor cable in his path. *U-47* hit it, pushing her towards the shore and forcing her aground. However, in anticipation of such an emergency, her ballast tanks were partly full and Prien blew them to gain buoyancy. Putting the rudder hard to port, with his port engine stopped and his starboard one running slow ahead, Prien freed the boat, the cable scraping along its hull.

His troubles were not yet over, for now a passing taxi's headlights shone on the U-boat's upper hull. The car stopped, reversed and drove off. It is said that the driver tried to warn the local police, but was not believed.

On board the battleship the watches changed at midnight. The broken Carley floats had been piled up in pieces on the fo'c'sle – not ideal in an emergency but better than nothing. *Daisy II*, having arrived with the ship's mail, was tied up against the battleship's port side. The night was cold and quiet. Those on *Royal Oak*'s bridge could make out the cliffs, about half a mile away, silhouetted against the sky.

Prien turned *U-47* to starboard, into Scapa Bay. Much of the anchorage was empty as most of the fleet had been withdrawn to Loch Ewe, on Scotland's west coast. HMS *Repulse* had left at five o'clock that afternoon for Rosyth. Although German Intelligence had realised this, it was now too late to inform Prien.

Just before one in the morning he saw *Royal Oak* ahead of him and a second ship. This was HMS *Pegasus*, which he misidentified as *Repulse*. Her size and profile were very different, but clearly Prien saw what he expected to see. *Royal Oak*'s starboard side was facing towards him. *U-47* was right in the heart of the enemy's anchorage and still nobody had raised the alarm. When within 4,000 yards, he fired four torpedoes, though only three left their tubes. Two headed towards *Royal Oak* and one towards *Pegasus*.

On board *Royal Oak* there was a small explosion, thought to be in a forward inflammable materials store, pitching some men out of their hammocks in the fo'c'sle. No one on watch took it for a torpedo. There was a roar as the anchor chains ran out. Although an investigation began, it seemed that whatever it was had occurred ahead of the collision bulkhead. Water was flooding into the damaged area, for air escaping through vents at high pressure made it impossible to hold a hand over them. No general alarm was raised and most of those in their hammocks remained there. The whole ship had been shaken, but her trim remained the same.

Dick Caldwell was lying on his bunk when he heard the first explosion. Going out to the cabin flat, he saw several officers debating where it could have occurred. After several minutes some men drifted back to their cabins.

Prien calmly turned and fired one of his boat's stern tubes. This missed, or had no effect. Having reloaded his bow tubes, he then turned and fired again.

This time two or three torpedoes struck *Royal Oak*'s starboard side. At once the battleship heeled over to starboard, and as she started to go down, water poured in through the plywood ventilators, accelerating the process.

Dick Caldwell heard glass tinkling in the silence that followed. Then the lights went out, the power failed, meaning that no orders could be given over the Tannoy, and a horrific fire started in an after magazine, sending burning cordite gas through the vents.

Anyone who has walked around HMS *Belfast* today knows how cramped space can be below decks and how easy it is to become disorientated. Some men burned to death in their hammocks, while others, with skin peeling off, staggered around screaming in the darkness, colliding with each other or with loose gear falling over them. A fortunate few, coughing from the gas, found companionways and open hatches, reaching the deck as it tilted over. Others unscrewed the ventilators and scrambled out through them.

Shocked but not scared, Dick Caldwell reached the deck clad in pyjamas, jacket and one left slipper. He could think only of the things left in his cabin. These included a new tennis racket, and a book he had borrowed, promising to return it. Then there was £3 in a drawer. It felt unreal, as in a film. As the ship tilted, he fell, then was thrown into the water.

Even now, someone tried to enforce discipline. On deck a braying 'county' voice called 'Wait for the word!' but a lot of men ignored him and promptly jumped straight into the Flow. Some dropped 20 feet, then swam madly to get away from the ship before her suction took them down with her. Their home, which until a few minutes ago had seemed so secure, was disappearing, pitching them into a black, oily, freezing nightmare.

Some had run across to the port side, boarding *Daisy II*. As *Royal Oak* tilted over the drifter was caught on top of the port torpedo blister. She went full astern, sliding off with a roar. It had all happened so quickly that there had been no time to launch most of the battleship's lifeboats and many of her crew lacked lifejackets. Her picket boat, intended to take fifty-five men, turned over after a hundred had scrambled onto it.

The battleship lurched, rolling right over, with a crash of shells and other equipment inside her. Over half of her crew were still trapped inside, one being Sick Berth Attendant Bendell, who tried to get out through a porthole in the pantry of the Petty Officers' Mess. Water poured in through it, but an air pocket formed, stopping the flow for a moment. He desperately dived for the porthole and after two attempts swam out through it, rising through the black water to the surface. Bendell may have been the last man to escape from *Royal Oak*.

For those who had been burned and were now in the water, there was no pain. That would come later, when others touched them. For now, to raise morale, survivors started singing 'Roll out the Barrel' or 'South of the Border'. This quickly changed to 'Daisy, Daisy' as the drifter came round to pick them up. Her skipper, John Gatt, would receive the Distinguished Service Cross. His crew saved 386 men that night, one of them Caldwell, who ended up shivering on a hot grating in the engine room. However, he could not find them all and others drifted away, dying of shock and hypothermia.

Some fifty men tried swimming for the shore, but less than half made it. The crew of HMS *Pegasus*, which had not been hit by the one torpedo aimed at her, did their best for the survivors once they had been alerted to what had happened. Hot drinks and baths were made available to the survivors, who also had oil scrubbed from them. The kindness later shown by people in Thurso would never be forgotten.

Prien turned away, returning through Kirk Sound. This time he took the wider southern gap, between the *Thames* and Lamb Holm. In so doing he passed over the fourth, completely sunken blockship, which the Germans had not been aware of. Struggling at full power against the incoming tide, Prien then narrowly avoided a jetty before he reached the open sea.

Following a hero's welcome at Wilhelmshaven, *U-47*'s crew were personally received by Hitler after a flight to Berlin and a triumphal march through the city. Prien was awarded the Knight's Cross, one of Germany's highest decorations, and all his men the Iron Cross, First or Second Class.

That night the crew attended a show at the Wintergarten variety theatre, where Prien was called on to make a speech, which the German broadcasting service promptly put on the air. This started a controversy, as what he said was disputed by those survivors who heard it. Prien still claimed to have hit *Repulse*, which was certainly not true, and to have aimed by the light of the Aurora Borealis, despite them stating that it was a completely dark night.

Many survivors believed that their ship had been sabotaged – a myth that grew when repeated. Some claimed the stores loaded that afternoon had had the words 'Royal Oak' pencilled on them, against regulations. The explosions – some said three and others four – had not sounded like torpedoes. Why had no torpedo tracks been seen by those on watch? If so many had been fired, where was the evidence?

U-47 returning to Kiel. (After The Battle)

Günther Prien in typically scruffy U-boat crew attire on *U-47*'s bridge, in conversation with some Luftwaffe personnel. (After The Battle)

After a shave and a change of uniform, Prien is congratulated by Hitler and Raeder. (IWM Neg. No. HU 40022)

Then there were the spy stories, which surfaced from 1942. There had been a 'sleeper' agent living in Orkney for years, supposedly as a Kirkwall watchmaker or innkeeper, who had been picked up by Prien that night and quietly returned to Germany. His information had guided *U-47* in. Prien had visited Orkney before the war, supposedly on holiday but actually spying while in the Hitler Youth. The taxi driver whose lights had shone on *U-47* had been an agent in the pay of the pro-Allied Admiral Wilhelm Canaris, head of the *Abwehr* counter-intelligence organisation, to frustrate Prien's mission.

None of this was true. The watchmaker's existence was denied by a real Kirkwall jeweller and by Dönitz's memoirs. Prien never mentioned any such holiday. In 1980 the likely driver was identified as one Robbie Tulloch, who that night had been running fares to a dance in St Mary's, on the Mainland close to Kirk Sound.

In 1939 two types of torpedo, the G7a and G7e, were available to the Kriegsmarine. The G7a was powered by compressed air, which left a stream of bubbles on the surface behind it. The electrically driven G7e did not, and it could only be fired from a U-boat. In 1973 divers recovered two German torpedo motors, one of which is now displayed in Stromness Museum. They were electrically driven. Prien had indeed torpedoed *Royal Oak,* even though he embroidered his account afterwards.

One thing the survivors did agree on was the short interval – about 12 minutes – between the first explosion and the later ones. Had the first been internal? Stores taken aboard would have been checked and signed for by an officer. Even if one of the crates had been unchecked and had contained a bomb, how could it have been timed to go off shortly before or during Prien's attack? Coincidence seems unlikely. Also, who could have planted it? The IRA made no claim.

At the time much blame was unjustifiably directed towards MI5, Britain's counter-intelligence service, apparently in an attempt to distract from the Admiralty's neglect of Scapa's defences. The Naval Intelligence Department and Special Branch followed up the Kirkwall agent rumour, but no evidence surfaced. The Admiralty's inquiry, whose results were eventually published, showed how inadequate the defences against underwater attack had been.

Since the war several authors have investigated the allegations of agents and saboteurs, but they too have found nothing to back them up. Also, surviving members of Prien's crew have confirmed that they really did enter Scapa Flow. By their accounts Prien was a braggart and riding the crest of the wave when he reached Berlin. Goebbels scored a major propaganda triumph and Prien was happy to be part of it, which disgusted his fellow officers.

The whole affair shows how myth can take over from reality. Prien could not be questioned later, for he and *U-47*, with some replacement crew members, were later depth-charged and sunk by the destroyer HMS *Wolverine* in 1941.

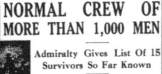

How the British press reacted to the news from Scapa Flow. (After The Battle)

✻   ✻   ✻

Nets were spread over the battleship's grave to catch any floating bodies, and others were recovered from the surrounding shores. Divers returned with horror stories of drowned men trapped halfway out of the portholes, their arms waving grotesquely in the dark water.

Commander Nichols had cheated death once more. Jack Wood's final letter to his family arrived on the day that they received official notification of his death. Dick Caldwell would go to sea again, aboard the battleship HMS *Prince of Wales*, and be sunk off Malaya in December 1941. He would survive that too.

The shock in Britain was considerable and a blow to the Navy's morale. Churchill's anger was hardly cooled by the news that within a week the blockship *Lake Neuchatel* had been sunk in Kirk Sound – a classic instance of shutting the stable door. Just to be sure, four other vessels were later added to the same area.

Having been in the job only a short while, he could not be held responsible for the Flow's neglected defences, although he faced some uncomfortable questioning when it emerged, not only that 833 lives had been lost, but also that some of them had been boy seamen of fifteen. Although Churchill saw the employment of boy volunteers as a valuable recruiting aid and was reluctant to alter the Navy's training system, from that time on nobody under the age of eighteen was allowed to serve on Royal Navy ships in wartime, unless exceptional circumstances were involved.

Perhaps those applied to Boy Seaman William Crawford, *Belfast*'s bemused diarist, who died aboard HMS *Hood* in May 1941. Just two months short of his eighteenth birthday, he was thought to have been the youngest member of her crew.

✻   ✻   ✻

Now the air war came to Orkney, one day after a Luftwaffe attack on warships at the Firth of Forth. At ten on the morning of 17 October four Junkers Ju 88 bombers of I/KG30 arrived. Two dived from high altitude, one of them damaging *Iron Duke*. The other was hit by the Lyness anti-aircraft guns and spun down to crash on Hoy. Its wireless operator, Unteroffizier F. Ambrosius, baled out, but his damaged parachute resulted in a heavy landing. The aircraft's bomb load exploded on impact, leaving so little trace that RAF Intelligence were at first unsure as to what it was. After a month in hospital, Ambrosius, by now fit enough to be interrogated, revealed it to have been a Ju 88.

Three hours later a second wave of fifteen Ju 88s, probably from the same unit, also attacked. This time their loads caused little damage, although one bomb fell uncomfortably close to a Belgian trawler in the Pentland Firth. One bomb exploded in a Hoy field while another landed on Flotta but failed to go off – the first bombs to fall on British soil during this war. Anti-aircraft fire brought down another Ju 88, this time into the sea between the islands of Hoy and Stroma. It was as well that the gunners were up to the mark, for 803 Squadron's Skuas were too slow to catch the enemy.

It was a clear day, with little cloud, and the battle could be seen from Wick on the Scottish mainland. Flak left a patchwork of black clouds across the sky, while colourful tracer soared skywards from the ships in deceptively slow, wobbling flight. For every shell that could be seen, there were many others that could not. The Orcadians turned out for the aerial spectacle, much as anyone might watch a football match, and children showed a marked reluctance to return to their classrooms.

Aboard *Iron Duke* it seemed for a moment like a rerun of *Royal Oak's* last moments. She listed 25 degrees to port as an exploding bomb flooded a boiler room. Again the lights went out and an order to abandon ship was given. However, she was safely beached in Ore Bay by the tug *St Martin*. The destroyer *Eskimo* provided power for her lights and pumps, but withdrew during the second raid. The Metal Industries Limited salvage crews, the successors to Cox & Danks in the High Seas Fleet recovery, patched her hull and pumped out the water. In December *Iron Duke* was beached again at Longhope, still leaking but at a rate the pumps could cope with, and continued in service as a depot ship for smaller vessels.

There were no raids during the long, dark winter, but the coming of spring brought new attacks. On 12 February the sirens sounded when two enemy aircraft appeared, apparently on reconnaissance as no bombs fell.

During these months the defences improved, with RAF airfields on Orkney becoming operational. By March there were eight coastal batteries, fifty anti-aircraft guns and 10,000 troops. The anti-submarine defences had also been strengthened. Scapa Flow now presented a better-prepared but still tempting target.

On 8 March Flying Officer Dutton of 111 Squadron, flying a Hurricane from RAF Wick, shot down a Ju 88 40 miles east of the Orkneys. Perhaps it had been carrying more than a camera, for a signal warned Admiral Forbes, on his way with the Home Fleet to reoccupy the Flow, that aircraft had dropped mines in the vicinity of Hoxa Sound.

This meant that the entry of the capital ships to the anchorage would be delayed while the channel was swept. Churchill, who was on board the battleship HMS *Rodney*, now transferred to a destroyer, arriving through Switha Sound. He was pleased to find the defences much improved since his last visit. The capital ships arrived safely after the minesweepers had carried out their dangerous work.

However, there were still defence problems. On 16 March radar in the Shetlands spotted an incoming raid, but the Netherbutton site failed to do so. Reported as fifteen Heinkel 111s, between them they dropped 121 high-explosive bombs and over 500 incendiaries, inflicting further damage on *Iron Duke* and the cruiser *Norfolk*.

Refuelling two 111 Squadron Hurricanes from an Albion bowser at RAF Wick in February 1940. (IWM Neg. No. CH64)

Living in a cottage at Bridge of Waithe, 10 miles west of Kirkwall, were James and Lily Isbister – a local Orkney surname. Their three-month-old son Neil was sleeping in his pram in the living room when the bombs started falling. The Isbisters pulled two passing women, Mrs Burnett and Miss Jane Muir, inside for shelter. Then a bomb struck the house of Miss Isabela Macleod across the road. As James ran out to help, another bomb killed him. Both houses were damaged but everyone else survived, the baby's pram being covered in broken glass. James Isbister, aged twenty-seven, was the first British civilian to die from enemy action during the Second World War.

In a reprisal, and as a change from leaflet raids, on the night of 19 March the RAF attacked the German seaplane base at Hornum on the island of Sylt – the first real raid on a German land target. However, it was still not total war, Hornum being selected because there was no nearby civilian housing. Out of fifty aircraft, one Whitley was lost and two others returned with damage. Most crews reported accurate bombing, but a photographic sortie by a Blenheim on the 27th showed little damage. German reports spoke of three men wounded by a hit on a sickbay and damage to a few aircraft. As if proof had been needed, this showed the ineffectiveness of night raids without adequate navigational facilities.

On 2 April KG30 attacked again, but the Ju 88s met heavy gunfire and did not press home their attack. One bomb caused three splinter casualties.

By now the Germans were preparing to invade Denmark and Norway, with further raids to cover this. On the evening of the 8th, He 111s of

James Isbister, the first British civilian killed in an air raid during the Second World War. (After The Battle)

A German incendiary bomb – small but deadly. (IWM D3534)

1 KG. INCENDIARY BOMB WITH EXPLOSIVE NOSE (I.B.E.N.)

WEIGHT, INCLUDING NOSE 2·2 KG.– NEARLY 5 LB

TAIL UNIT

ARMING WIRE ⑫

INCENDIARY UNIT

DIA. 2"

20¾"

SAFETY PIN ⑬

FUZE BODY

DELAYED ACTION EXPLOSIVE UNIT

ARMING WIRE ⑫–13" LONG WITH A METAL DISC ⑭ 1½" DIA. AT THE TOP, PASSES THROUGH THE TAIL DRUM AND THROUGH A HOLE IN THE SAFETY PIN ⑬. ON RELEASE FROM THE AIR-CRAFT, AIR PRESSURE ON THE DISC WITHDRAWS THE WIRE FROM THE SAFETY PIN, WHICH IS EJECTED BY A SPRING.

WHEN THE BOMB LANDS, THE STRIKER ① FIRES THE DETONATOR ② WHICH IGNITES BOTH THE CAP ③ & THE FLASH-TRAIN ④.

THE FLASH FROM THE CAP ③ FIRES THE MAIN INCENDIARY FILLING ⑤ WHICH EVENTUALLY IGNITES THE INFLAMMABLE ALLOY CASE ⑥ OF THE INCENDIARY UNIT.

MEANWHILE THE FLASH-TRAIN ④ SETS OFF THE TIME FUZE ⑦.

THIS BURNS SLOWLY FOR UP TO 7 MINUTES, AND THEN FIRES A SECOND DETONATOR ⑧ WHICH DETONATES THE MAIN EXPLOSIVE CHARGE ⑨.

THE MAIN EXPLOSIVE CHARGE IS CARRIED IN A STEEL CONTAINER ⑩ WHICH BURSTS INTO MANY FRAGMENTS WHEN THE CHARGE ⑨ DETONATES.

THE THIN METAL NOSE-COVER ⑪ IS NOT ALWAYS FOUND ON THE BOMB.

MINISTRY OF HOME SECURITY
INSPECTOR GENERAL'S DEPARTMENT
INCENDIARY BOMB INSTRUCTIONAL DIAGRAM Nº 3.

Crown Copyright Reserved

An incendiary bomb's workings explained by the Ministry of Home Security. Some were booby-trapped with small explosive charges. (After The Battle)

KG26 came. This time the radar warning was timely, four aircraft being claimed by the Scapa barrage and three by the Hurricanes of 43 Squadron, scrambled from Wick. Six bombs were scattered across the islands. Earth buried a civilian who was unhurt but suffered from shock, while a family escaped injury when their farmhouse roof was hit. Incendiary bombs caused several heather fires.

Two Heinkels ditched after combat, but the third, damaged by Sergeant Herbert Hallowes, made a landing at Wick that nobody who saw it would ever forget. Following it down was 43's commanding officer, Squadron Leader Peter Townsend, who was interviewed on BBC 1's *Simon Dee Show* in the late 1960s:

> He apparently thought it was a waterfield. Anyway, he got the green and crash-landed. The bomber came to a halt, the hatch opened, a dinghy dropped out, two Germans got into it and started trying to row across the runway!

The audience fell about laughing. Leutnant K. Weigel and Oberfeldwebel B. Rehbein did not find it so amusing at the time, especially as their two comrades lay dead in the aircraft.

There would be a further attack on the Flow on 10 April, by which time the Scandinavian invasion had started, with a few other incidents as the war continued, but these fall outside the confines of this book.

To reinforce the blockships and improve communications, Italian prisoners were subsequently brought in to build four causeways linking the eastern islands. These became collectively known as the Churchill Barriers. Causeway No. 1 now crosses Kirk Sound, making any repeat of Prien's manoeuvres impossible. Anyone driving between the islands can still see the remains of the blockships, although some have collapsed, leaving only a small amount of rusty metal above the surface.

Ships would come and go until the White Ensign was hauled down in 1957. Lyness base's refuelling facilities finally closed in 1976. Neither Prien nor his fellow U-boat captains ever returned.

Today, the causeways, and a fine chapel built from a Nissen hut, remain as memorials to those prisoners who, far from Italy's sunny skies, spent years in this bleak but beautiful part of the world. Museums at Lyness and Kirkwall illustrate the impact two world wars had on the community.

Royal Oak's ship's bell is displayed in St Magnus Cathedral in Kirkwall. A green wreck buoy marks her position. As she is classed as a war grave, diving on her is forbidden, except for Royal Navy divers who annually tie a White Ensign to the wreck. These flags were subsequently given, first to the relatives of her dead crew and, in more recent times, to other families who have lost relatives serving in the Navy. She lies on her side, with oil still coming up from her.

5

SONS OF THE WAVES

There are two ways in which England may be afflicted. One is by invasion.
The other is by impeachment of her trades.

Sir Walter Raleigh

The menace of the German magnetic mine loomed large in the first six months of the war, but it had come about as the result of British developments in the previous war. The spherical horned contact mine, anchored to float on or just below the surface, had been well known since the latter part of the nineteenth century. It was simple in design, with few moving parts to go wrong. Examples of this weapon, usually painted red with a sailors' charity collecting box now added, can be seen around the British coast from Scarborough to Studland.

The magnetic mine was more recent, having been first deployed by the Royal Navy in 1918 against U-boat bases along the Belgian coast. This type lay below the water's surface, exploding when a ship's hull passing over it caused a change in the magnetic field around it. However, they had failed to function as intended, going off harmlessly beside ships instead of below them.

In the interwar period there was little British interest in mines – it was said that senior officers considered this weapon to be the resort of second-class naval powers. However, for the Germans, getting it to work correctly presented a problem that they were determined to solve. The Kriegsmarine's Barrage Research Department, secretly working at the port of Kiel, developed a magnetic detonator under the camouflage of 'a rangefinder for balloons'. By 1930 the first fifty were available.

Contact mines, being moored in shallow water, could be cut adrift by a minesweeper, brought to the surface and then destroyed by gunfire. The magnetic mine, resting on the seabed, could not be swept in this fashion. Although the shock was reduced in deep water, when laid in coastal regions and river estuaries, at depths of less than 100 feet, its effect would prove devastating.

From the day war broke out the Kriegsmarine had begun to lay contact mines, which claimed their first two victims, the steam ships *Magdapur* and *Goodwood*, on 10 September. Mines could be laid by destroyers, E-boats or by aircraft such as the Heinkel 111, the Ju 88 and the He 115 seaplane. Minelaying U-boats were particularly active, and the Appendix at the end of this book shows how successful they were.

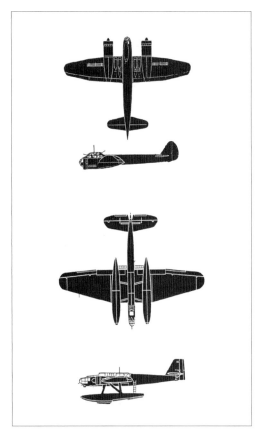

Recognition silhouettes of the Junkers Ju 88A-1 and the Heinkel He 115 seaplane, both of which were involved in reconnaissance and mine-laying at this time.

The magnetic mine's first victim was the Dutch liner *Simon Bolivar* in the North Sea on 19 November, with the loss of eighty-three lives. The Royal Navy lost the destroyers *Blanche* and *Gypsy*, the latter breaking in two between her funnels off Harwich. The destroyer HMS *Griffin* went to her aid in the dark, picking up survivors to the mournful toll of a channel bell buoy. The minelaying cruiser *Adventure* had been damaged, as had the cruiser *Belfast*, which fell victim to a mine laid in the Firth of Forth by *U-21*. One man died and fifteen were injured. The cruiser's back was broken and scrapping was considered, but such was the demand for new vessels that she was laid up for repairs until October 1942, perhaps surviving because of that.

During November the situation had become serious, with the Port of London all but closed. On the evening of the 21st an Army sentry at an artillery range near Shoeburyness, on a desolate stretch of the Essex coast, heard a German aircraft approaching. He identified it as a Heinkel 111, though some accounts say it was the earlier and by now obsolete He 59 biplane. He saw an object on a parachute, described as 'looking like an Army kitbag', land just offshore. The crew had made the mistake of dropping the mine too close in.

This sighting was reported to the Admiralty, who passed it on to HMS *Vernon*, the Mine and Torpedo School at Portsmouth. Lieutenant Commander

The destroyer HMS *Blanche*, lost to a magnetic mine in the Thames estuary on 13 November 1939. (IWM)

The cruiser HMS *Belfast* – an early victim of the magnetic mine. (IWM Neg. No. MH29235)

John Ouvry, an expert in non-contact mines, joined torpedoman Lieutenant Commander Roger Lewis at the Admiralty. Arriving at Shoeburyness by car at half past three on the morning of the 23rd, they met Commander Bowles, the naval officer in charge, at Southend's Palace Hotel, to be told the tide was ebbing and that the object should be visible by low water, at four o'clock.

Acute strain was being caused by these weapons. The Thames and Humber estuaries had been mined, as had the channel at Harwich, and any ships waiting offshore were obvious targets for Luftwaffe attack. Several were anchored off Southend, waiting for the channel to be cleared. One of them had already been damaged as the tide's turning caused her to swing at anchor. At Shoeburyness the three officers met Commander Maton, the Naval Experimental Officer on the gunnery range, with a party of soldiers.

This was – literally – a step in the dark, as it was not yet known whether the mine was magnetic or acoustic. Lewis and Ouvry, having removed all metal from their uniforms and pockets as a precaution, followed the sentry who had witnessed the drop across the mudflats. Maton's party of soldiers followed at a safe distance. On seeing a sinister black shape, the soldiers were sent back, leaving the officers, with two photographers, to walk on through darkness and rain. Not for nothing is this known to those engaged in bomb disposal as 'the longest walk in the world'.

Buried slightly nose down in the wet sand, the mine was cylindrical, one end being domed with tubular horns sticking out, while the other tapered to a circular opening, with a large phosphor-bronze spring inside. An examination by torchlight followed, revealing, as Ouvry's report later stated, 'two unpleasant looking fittings near the fore end and these looked like being our Public Enemies Nos 1 and 2'.

The Shoeburyness magnetic mine, photographed at first light as the tide receded. (IWM)

One was evidently a hydrostatic valve, which was encouraging, but the other was something quite unrecognisable made of polished aluminium and secured by a screwed ring sealed with tallow. Here again was some encouragement, for there was what appeared to be a 'tear off' strip somewhat twisted but still firmly secured to it and possibly a safety arrangement. This latter fitting seemed the more likely to harbour a primer and detonator and so I decided that it should be the first to be tackled.

As a four-pin spanner would be needed to unscrew this securing ring, Lewis took an impression on a signal pad. Commander Maton had a brass – therefore non-magnetic – spanner made in his workshop by noon, as the site would be uncovered again soon after. The photographers then recorded the mine from different angles.

After breakfast at Maton's house, a report came that a second mine was now visible, some 300 yards from the first – aircraft dropped them in pairs. A preliminary report, with copies of the first photographs, went to the Admiralty. It must have occurred to Lewis and Ouvry that if anything went wrong this would be all the record their Lordships would have.

By one o'clock that afternoon both mines were visible. Maton and his soldiers took up a sheltered position on the foreshore nearby, accompanied by a tractor lorry with a crane. Lewis and Ouvry examined the second mine while the photographer took daylight shots of the first one. A mine recovery team arrived from HMS *Vernon*, with other non-magnetic tools. Ouvry, as the most experienced officer, walked out with Chief Petty Officer C. E. Baldwin to tackle the first mine. Lewis, with Able Seaman A. L. Vearncombe, remained behind to observe from a distance. A sequence of events had been arranged, just in case the first team made a mistake.

To fit the special spanner it was necessary to bend the copper strip to one side. Though told to handle it carefully, Baldwin pulled too hard and it nearly came off. Quickly stopping him, Ouvry fitted the pin spanner and started to unscrew the ring. Having found the fitting would come free, but thinking it might be a magnetic needle, Ouvry carefully lifted the cylinder he found free of the mine, taking three minutes to do so.

The cylinder turned out to be a detonator, with discs of explosive, as primers for the main charge, beneath it. This cylinder had been fitted in anticipation of the mine being dropped on land, and the copper strip was an igniter for a delayed-action fuse.

To reach those fittings buried in the sand, Lewis and Vearncombe came across to turn the mine over, using a rope. A plate was unscrewed, revealing a circular screwed bung. Ouvry reported, 'As there was no suitable spanner available some force had to be used to move it. Another screwed plate was exposed to view with two terminals mounted on it with a pair of leads leading from them and away out of sight through a hole in the side of the casing.'

Having parted the leads and unscrewed the plate with a non-magnetic screwdriver, this turned out to be the carrier of an electric detonator of

the type used on German contact mines. At last Ouvry felt on familiar
ground. Two primers and a hydrostatic valve were removed, though as
one detonator was being carried ashore it began to tick. It later became
clear that a clock in the fitting they had removed from under the mine was
actuated by water pressure, being designed to keep the mine safe after it
had dropped to the seabed. Fortunately for Ouvry and Baldwin the clock
had jammed – otherwise the mine would have been fully armed by the time
it was discovered.

Armed with his colleagues' knowledge, Lieutenant J. E. M. Glenny
defused the second mine. On 19 December the King would visit HMS
Vernon to present the first naval awards of this war. Lewis and Ouvry
received the DSO, and Glenny the DSC. Baldwin and Vearncombe received
DSMs. The George Cross and George Medal, later instituted for bravery
while not under fire, would not be available until September 1940.

Now safe, though still containing 660 pounds of explosive, the mine
was taken by lorry to HMS *Vernon*, for examination in a non-magnetic
laboratory. It contained no booby trap – lucky again, as the room was full
of interested officers at the time. However, the question as to whether it was
magnetic was still unanswered. Churchill, characteristically, had ordered
work to proceed night and day until this problem had been solved.

A well-earned DSO for
Lieutenant Commander
Ouvry from the King.
(IWM Neg. No. MH739)

Removal of the rear plate and the rubber dome behind it showed a scale with the word 'gauss' – the unit of a magnetic field. The mechanism was removed and the main charge steamed out of the mine. Within eighteen hours Admiralty scientists had solved the riddle of how it worked.

In the northern hemisphere, a horizontally balanced magnetic needle will dip down towards the earth's magnetic field. The mine had a bar magnet pivoted and biased by a helical spring, keeping the north pole upwards. The spring kept open a contact on this pole, its strength being adjustable, so balancing the vertical component of the earth's magnetic field at the point where the mine was to be laid. This one had been set at 0.02 gauss. As the actuator was set in gimbals, irrespective of how the mine rested on the seabed, the magnet remained in the correct position, the spring counteracting the north-seeking pole's tendency to dip downward.

It is part of any child's first physics lesson that like poles repel and unlike poles attract. When a ship passing overhead repelled the mine's north pole, the spring was overcome, closing an electrical contact to explode the mine. However, any ship built in the southern hemisphere would have its magnetism reversed and could therefore sail over the mine with impunity.

This now being sorted out, what was to be done about it? The first solution was HMS *Borde*, the world's first magnetic minesweeper. She carried a 400-ton electromagnet, made up from a bundle of railway lines 200 feet long. The first mine detonated by this strange vessel went off on Christmas Eve 1939, but the shock was such that to avoid broken ankles everyone on board had to stand on thick layers of rubber.

No ship could stand that kind of punishment indefinitely, and in November 1939 German naval stores held no less than 20,000 mines. Sweeping from the air seemed the answer, but Air Marshal Sir Wilfred Freeman, the Air Member for Development and Production, sought to avoid current bomber output being disrupted. He would have preferred the Handley Page Harrow, by now an obsolete bomber, or the Armstrong Whitworth Ensign airliner to be converted for this new role, but he was overruled.

So it was that the Vickers Wellington, the best of the RAF's bombers at this time, was put to a use that its designer, Barnes Wallis, could never have foreseen. The Vickers factory at Weybridge in Surrey, by the famous Brooklands racetrack, now had the job of fitting a Wellington with a 51-foot-diameter electromagnetic ring, attached under the wings and fuselage. This contained a paper-insulated aluminium strip coil, energised by a 35-kW generator powered by a Ford V8 engine mounted in the aircraft's rear fuselage. Wags dubbed it 'the Halo' or 'the Electric Doughnut'.

A Mark IA, P2516, was taken from the production line and drastically modified. Out went the gun turrets, radio and any other unnecessary weight, to provide space for the bulky generator and V8. George Edwards, who had joined Vickers as a draughtsman in 1935 and was beginning to make a name for himself, tackled the aircraft modifications while Wallis

A DWI Wellington. The ring's size must have given even the most experienced of pilots pause for thought. (Author's collection)

worked on the problems of carrying such a large device, with its inevitable effect on the Wellington's compass.

George Edwards had previously worked as an engineer in London's docks and, coming from such a background, had a habit of saying what he thought. So did Trevor Westbrook, who had been brought in from Supermarine to get the Vickers factory moving. Both had the job of adapting the B9/32 prototype from the paragon of geodetic construction that Wallis had designed into what, from the RAF's point of view, was the more practical Wellington Mark I. Wallis, a far tougher character than Michael Redgrave's mild-mannered old buffer in *The Dam Busters*, was someone determined to get his own way. Arguments had flared between them, to the point where Paul Wyand, the Chief Draughtsman, had had to talk George Edwards out of giving up altogether:

> The most exciting job that I did around that time was the minesweeping Wellington. I got given the job of doing it when Wallis was running it. The pressures were out of this world. Poor old Wallis went sick – I got stuck with the job of coping with it. Westbrook came along and said, 'Now, you used to do a bit of putting together outside as well as laying about on a drawing-board and doing the drawing, didn't you?' and I said, yes, I did. 'Well,' he said, 'the pressure on me with this thing is so great that there's no way we're going to do this in the ordinary orthodox way of running it. You really are going to have to go down in the factory and run this thing at the same time that you're coping with it in the Drawing Office.' And he said, 'I mean at the

same time. I don't mean that you're going to abandon the Drawing Office and go down in the factory, you're going to have to do it both ends.'

And I slept a bit – one of my gags of late used to be that every night I had to send a set of photographs up to Churchill, who was then First Lord of the Admiralty, to show him what I had done the night before. And, as I've said often, in modern times they'd need a set of photographs at three-monthly intervals for anybody to be able to see that anybody had done anything. But I had to demonstrate each night that I'd done something since the night before.

Anyway, we got the thing done and it worked. And it was only when I read Churchill's life story covering that period that I realised what a fearful menace the magnetic mines were, although I was having it rammed down my throat night and day while we were doing this job. We could damn near have lost the war if something hadn't been done.

Having worked all the way through Christmas 1939, with little sleep, George Edwards found himself in a new job – that of Experimental Manager at Weybridge. It was a stepping stone to greater things, as he became Chief Designer after the war, being knighted for his work on the Viscount airliner, and ultimately realising his long-term ambition of running the Weybridge factory.

During December a further four Wellingtons were taken from the line for modification, with the proviso that any further requirements would be met by a sub-contractor – Rollasons at Croydon Airport, which had now become an RAF base. To fly them, 1 General Reconnaissance Unit – a deliberately misleading title – was formed at RAF Manston in Kent, followed by two others in Norfolk and Hampshire. These Wellingtons were designated Vickers Type 418, and described as 'Directional Wireless Installation' aircraft – another bit of flimsy camouflage that seems to have fooled nobody.

By now known as the DWI Mark I, P2516 was test-flown with an initially empty ring casing by the Vickers Chief Test Pilot, Joseph 'Mutt' Summers, on 21 December at the Aeroplane and Armament Experimental Establishment at Boscombe Down in Wiltshire. For two hours Summers flew over the Shoeburyness mine's mechanism at heights from 10 to 100 feet, while the scientists checked the polar diagram of the aircraft's magnetic field. As the mine's magnet clicked away, it was concluded that the idea was practicable.

Operational flights began in January 1940, the first over the Medway estuary in Kent. As soon as the ring was switched on a mine blew up. The aircraft handled well on takeoff and was steady in flight, so that maintaining a height of 30 to 40 feet over water was no problem. Exploding a mine had little effect either – except on 13 January when one aircraft flew low near a wreck off the North Goodwin Sands, detonating a mine which recorded over 10g on an accelerometer in the tail. Although hatches were blown off, a check revealed no structural damage, which said much for the Wellington's design.

The aircraft was unarmed and heavier when turning, as the ring weighed over two tons and, unlike a bomb load, could not be got rid of. When coming in to land, it caused drag and pilots were told that once they had settled to their approach speed they were to land whatever the circumstances. Going round again was prohibited, in case they lost speed and stalled.

Calculations showed that the magnetic field could be amplified by up to 50 per cent without increasing the hazard to the aircraft. Rollasons modified a further batch of eleven Wellington Mark Is at Croydon as DWI Mark IIs, using a more powerful English Electric generator driven by a Gypsy Six aircraft engine. This enabled a smaller 48-foot-diameter ring to be used. Some were used later in the war to sweep the Suez Canal. The Germans copied the idea, using Ju 52s.

Although successful, the DWI Wellingtons only swept a narrow and unmarked channel. A better long-term solution was the Double L sweep, which consisted of two wooden-hulled ships steaming 300 yards apart. Each towed two lengths of floating cable, one a third of a mile long and the other shorter. The electrodes at the end of each cable received DC 5-second pulses at 3,000 amperes – one cable for the negative pole, the other for the positive. The salt water between the electrodes completed the electrical circuit. This set up an intense 10-acre magnetic field in the water, exploding mines within it. Special wooden-hulled minesweepers were commissioned and proved successful.

By February 1940 the Double L was in use, destroying seventy-four mines in that first month alone. A further countermeasure was to 'degauss' a ship by passing direct current through a heavy cable wound round its hull. A variation on this was to 'wipe' a ship's magnetic signature by drawing a cable carrying several thousand amperes up the side of its hull. The current made it cling to the metal, reversing the ship's natural magnetism. This technique would be used on 'the little ships' at Dunkirk, of which only two were lost to magnetic mines.

By the summer of 1940 a weapon that might have won the war, at least at sea, was beaten. The Luftwaffe came to the same conclusion, hence the 'landmines' dropped on London and other cities the following autumn.

*   *   *

Although the U-boat would turn out to be the primary threat to Britain's sea trade, in this first year of war German surface raiders would play a part as well. A severe shortage of ships had led the Royal Navy to convert a number of liners to armed merchant cruisers. It was an inadequate response, but a ship on patrol, however ill-suited, was better than no ship at all.

One such was the former P&O liner *Rawalpindi*, commanded by Captain Edward Kennedy. A veteran, nearly sixty years old, who had faced retirement after the First World War, he had enthusiastically responded to a recall to duty. His ship had been armed with 6-inch guns, which, he told a friend, he had every intention of using.

Rawalpindi had first come close to the enemy at the time of Prien's entry into Scapa Flow, but, as Captain Kennedy later commented, 'He was after bigger fish than us.' Now, as November dawned, she was part of the Northern Patrol – enforcing the Navy's North Sea blockade by intercepting German merchant vessels between the Faroe Islands, Iceland and Norway. Already she had boarded the German ship *Gonzenheim*, sinking her after taking her crew prisoner. It was not surprising that in one of his letters home Captain Kennedy wrote that he was as contented as any man could be.

Rawalpindi left the Clyde again during this month to resume her patrol, enduring a week of vile weather. On the evening of 22 November a concert was staged by her crew, most of them reservists, to which her skipper contributed a song. It was decided to stage it again the following day for the benefit of those who had been on watch at the time.

Next morning they sighted a Swedish ship. Although it was neutral, the possibility of contraband cargo led a boarding officer, Sub-Lieutenant Anderson, with an armed guard, to sail it to a British port. He had tossed a coin with his fellow officer, Lieutenant Pickersgill, for the honour, and Pickersgill had lost.

HMS *Rawalpindi*.

There would be no more show performances. As the sky darkened at 1600 that afternoon a ship was sighted 7 miles away. The battlecruisers *Scharnhorst* and *Gneisenau* had left Wilhelmshaven two days earlier under the command of Admiral Wilhelm Marschall. Making for the Atlantic, they had passed undetected to the north of the Shetland and Faroe Islands.

At first neither recognised the other. *Scharnhorst*'s foretop lookout reported a steamer on their starboard beam. Kapitän zur See Kurt Cesar Hoffmann climbed up to see for himself. Though he considered it to be an armed merchant cruiser, he was cautious. It might be neutral. Having informed his admiral by radio, he ordered his ship to action stations.

Captain Kennedy, initially thinking he had found another blockade runner, mustered a second boarding party under Pickersgill. The latter, thinking his hour had come, changed his mind when he realised this was a warship, with modern 11-inch guns that outranged their elderly armament. There was only one chance – head towards the darkening eastern horizon, hoping to blend with it before the Germans came within range, although this would have made little difference as the German ships, carrying Seetakt radar, could still have fired accurately in the dark.

Hoffmann signalled, 'What ship? Origin and where bound? Stop and do not use wireless.' The response was 'FAM' – a meaningless call sign, but her next actions left no doubt as to her nationality. Had *Rawalpindi* still been a merchant ship, no one would have blamed her crew had they surrendered. However, she now flew the White Ensign and that meant something to everyone on board, especially her skipper. Moving away at her full speed of 17 knots, she released smoke floats while her wireless operator put out a signal: 'Immediate. Am being chased by battleship.'

The battlecruiser *Gneisenau*. (IWM)

The Home Fleet had just returned to the Clyde when this signal was received. 'Enemy is *Deutschland*.' Captain Kennedy did not know that this pocket battleship was in port at the time.

At 1700 the battle began. *Scharnhorst*'s first two salvoes fell short, but her third and fourth proved deadly. *Rawalpindi*'s bridge took a direct hit, probably killing everyone on it, as did her wireless and generating rooms. The lights went out and there was no power for the ammunition hoists. Despite this and the fires that raged, *Rawalpindi*, her battle ensigns flying, fired back with anything available, causing some splinter casualties when a shell landed on *Scharnhorst*'s quarterdeck. Then *Gneisenau* approached on her other side and the crossfire that followed ended in those who were able abandoning ship.

Some sixty men under Lieutenant Pickersgill made for three boats at the stern, in which forty escaped. One still aboard signalled, 'Please send boats.' Although unable to do so due to the rough seas, both ships manoeuvred alongside those that had got away. *Gneisenau* picked up twenty-one men from one boat and *Scharnhorst* six from another. The third was left behind when Marschall signalled, 'Cease picking up survivors immediately. Follow me.'

Gneisenau's lookouts had seen the cruiser HMS *Newcastle*, which had responded to *Rawalpindi*'s last signals. Her captain tried to shadow them until the Home Fleet arrived, but lost them in a rainstorm. Marschall was, it seems, quite happy to sink an old liner but not to face a more modern British warship.

The Home Fleet sailed within hours, some ships making for *Rawalpindi*'s last position while others headed north-east, seeking to intercept the enemy between the Shetlands and Norway. However, Marschall eluded them, heading north to await suitable weather before passing through their patrol lines on the 26th. He reached home the next day, but had not carried out his plan to attack British shipping in the Atlantic. One German sailor later commented that this affair left 'a nasty taste in the mouth'.

On the 24th *Rawalpindi*'s sister ship *Chitral* found the third boat, rescuing ten men, and one spreadeagled over another upturned vessel, who survived despite having been in that position for several hours. Captain Kennedy was lost with 263 of his crew.

It is part of the British character to glory in gallant defeat. The unequal battle made inspiring newspaper copy, and Chamberlain praised the crew in the House of Commons. Mrs Kennedy received a unique parchment letter of appreciation from the Admiralty, whose First Lord unveiled a plaque to her husband at a High Wycombe church. A suggested VC award was not made, but the subsequent granting of grace-and-favour accommodation to his widow at Hampton Court was of more use.

On 29 November *U-35* was depth-charged by three British destroyers east of the Shetlands, surfacing long enough for all of her crew to be taken prisoner, which made them particularly fortunate. They were subsequently transferred to the Tower of London. In a routine that would become familiar across the world over the next six years, they were counted each day, and the catering turned out to be mixed. Years later one man recalled that the bacon they received was good, but his friend commented, 'Cabbage left, right and centre. English food in England? I wouldn't have called it food.' Their skipper Korvettenkapitän Werner Lott, complained about the conditions to such a degree that Captain Lord Louis Mountbatten, no less, had calmed him down by taking him, on parole, to Scott's restaurant in London!

It would have been a relief when, due to overcrowding, the POW camp within the Tower closed in December 1939, its inmates moving from the Tower Armouries to northern England and then Canada in 1941. In future it would be used only for very high-ranking prisoners, although nobody could have foreseen how important the next one would be.

The Navy was beginning to get results, which was more than could be said for Coastal Command, whose aircraft seemed particularly keen to attack friendly submarines, including *Seahorse*, *Seawolf* and *Sterlet*, though in each case fortunately without loss. This occurred despite the escort of outward-bound and returning submarines or the designation of exercise areas. It was due to poor navigation and the reluctance of submarine commanders to use recognition flares when attacked, in case a real enemy should spot them.

During December an Anson attacked what it took to be a U-boat off the west coast of Scotland. A 100-pound anti-submarine bomb hit squarely on the base of the conning tower. It did no more than shatter four light bulbs inside, which was as well since the submarine concerned was HMS *Snapper*. Things would not improve until the Anson was packed off to training and heavier, long-range aircraft arrived, with depth charges.

It was also during this month that HMS *Triumph* had an astonishing escape. Despite hitting a mine, which blew her bows off, her internal torpedo bulkheads held and she limped home. It is said that a rating in the fore ends slept throughout the incident! Success came on 4 December when HMS *Salmon* torpedoed *U-36* off Stavanger – the first of thirty-nine enemy submarines lost to British ones in this war.

Throughout this period British submariners had not achieved much, but they had proved they could operate off enemy coastal waters under the threat of aircraft or surface attack. The next time the Navy hit the headlines it would be under very different circumstances.

6

THE RIVER PLATE

If the worst happens, bring my sons up to be men.
Commodore Henry Harwood in a letter to his wife

In 1922, in an attempt to prevent another arms race, the Washington Agreement had laid down restrictions on future warship construction. Ships had been divided into two categories – capital ships with guns greater than 20-cm calibre, and smaller ships with guns of lesser calibre and displacement of not more than 10,000 tons.

Although Germany had not been invited, it was clear that she would be expected to abide by the terms. The ingenuity of her ship designers resulted in a large cruiser, which met the displacement limit but mounted six 28-cm (11-inch) guns in two triple turrets. The three vessels that would be built were classified as *Panzerschiffe* – armoured ships – a designation chosen to denote that Germany was keeping within the limits of the Versailles Treaty. However, they would become known around the world as 'pocket battleships'. Launched between 1931 and 1934, they were, in succession, the *Deutschland*, the *Admiral Scheer* and the *Admiral Graf Spee*.

The *Graf Spee* had taken part in three of the so-called neutrality patrols during the Spanish Civil War. Making the customary round of pre-war courtesy visits to foreign ports, she had lain at anchor off Spithead in May 1937, during King George VI's Coronation Naval Review, close to ships that in just over two years' time would be hunting for her. She had been part of the naval force when Hitler occupied Memel and on 21 August had left Wilhelmshaven, heading north-west, unseen, into the Atlantic, to turn south. Her task would be to raid Britain's commerce, taking on further fuel, when needed, from a tanker, the *Altmark*.

On 3 September she was 650 miles north-west of the Cape Verde Islands when a wireless telegraphist reported to the bridge that he had intercepted an uncoded signal on a British wavelength. There were just two words – 'Total Germany'. Confirmation from the *Seekriegsleitung* – the German Admiralty – followed. The crew were summoned on deck, to be told by their skipper, Kapitän zur See Hans Langsdorff, that they were now at war.

On the 26th *Graf Spee* and her sister ship *Deutschland*, which had also slipped into the Atlantic before the Royal Navy had covered its approaches, were both given freedom of action by Berlin. Langsdorff picked the South Atlantic trade routes as his hunting ground. Off Pernambuco *Graf Spee* first made her presence known when she met the tramp steamer *Clement* on 30 September.

The *Clement*'s skipper, Captain Harris, assuming the ship was the British cruiser HMS *Ajax*, went to his cabin to don a fresh white uniform. As he emerged, an Arado Ar 196 seaplane dived, firing a warning. Keeping his head, Harris stopped his ship, lowered the boats and told his wireless operator to send an SOS. Far from preventing this, Langsdorff got the Pernambuco transmitting station to broadcast a message on the 600-metre band, requesting the rescue of the crew from their boats. As a touch of deception he had the message signed '*Admiral Scheer*'. His other sister ship was nowhere near the scene, but it would offset the British and French superiority in numbers if several of their ships chased across the South Atlantic in search of one that was not there.

To add to this, when Captain Harris and his chief engineer were brought aboard, they saw the title '*Admiral Scheer*' painted over in grey. 'I'm sorry, Captain,' said Langsdorff, 'but I've got to sink your ship. We are, you see, at war.'

It could hardly have been more politely expressed. Langsdorff was a man of honour, a product of the old Imperial German Navy who had never been seen to give a Nazi salute. His humanity was to earn him respect from his enemies over the next three months. It must have felt unreal to Harris, standing on a German bridge, to watch while two torpedoes passed,

The pocket battleship *Deutschland*, photographed pre-war. (IWM Neg. No. HU1033)

farcically, under his ship. Finally the *Clement* went down, but only after the chief gunnery officer had used the main armament. 'She's a damned tough ship!' Harris said proudly.

A few hours later *Graf Spee* stopped the Greek steamer *Papelemos*. As her country was neutral – for now – and her cargo not suspect, the two British officers were transferred to her. It was then reported that the *Admiral Scheer* was roaming the South Atlantic.

As calculated, this astonished the British Admiralty. How had the *Scheer* appeared so quickly in the South Atlantic, only weeks after the RAF had targeted her at Wilhelmshaven? Admiral Sir Dudley Pound, the First Sea Lord, reacted exactly as his opposite number, Grossadmiral Erich Raeder, had anticipated. From 5 October eight hunting groups, twenty-two warships in all, were formed, to cover the whole Atlantic, seeking out the raiders.

Raeder was pleased. It all kept the Royal Navy guessing. This diversion meant withdrawing vessels from the Home Fleet, making it easier for other German ships to break out into the Atlantic.

Langsdorff continued to pick off solitary British merchantmen, taking advantage of the fact that the convoy system was only just beginning and that the British Merchant Navy, one of the largest in the world, with ships scattered all over it trying to get home, would remain vulnerable for months to come. He criss-crossed the South Atlantic, his victims being the *Ashlea*, the *Newton Beech*, the *Huntsman* and the *Trevanion*. Three weeks later Langsdorff appeared again, this time 2,000 miles away, sinking the tanker *Africa Shell* off what is now Mozambique. Langsdorff headed north, deliberately close to a Dutch liner so its passengers could photograph him, then south. He was proud of the fact that so far he had not taken a single British life, the crews either being allowed to row to the nearest shore, or taken on board *Graf Spee*, to be transferred at the first opportunity to the *Altmark* as more fuel was pumped aboard.

Meanwhile, fourteen warships of the Royal and French navies, uncertain whether they were pursuing one raider or two, ploughed through miles of empty sea from the North Atlantic to the Indian Ocean. One of the hunting groups so employed was the South American Squadron, which consisted of the three cruisers *Ajax*, *Achilles* and *Exeter*, under Commodore Henry Harwood. That month *Exeter* was due for a refit at Durban, and Harwood transferred his flag to *Ajax*, which as things turned out was as well for him. He had a sense that trouble was imminent, though this was not shared by *Exeter*'s crew, to whom the war seemed a long way off.

Langsdorff's luck began to run out when he sank the *Doric Star* on 2 December off Walvis Bay in South-West Africa. Before she went down, her wireless operator sent a message that was picked up by the British naval base at Simonstown in South Africa. It was also intercepted by Force K – the aircraft carrier *Ark Royal* and the battlecruiser *Renown*. This showed that the raider was on the Cape–Freetown route. *Exeter* was recalled, going to Port Stanley in the Falkland Islands for a four-day self-refit.

Commodore Henry Harwood, probably photographed aboard HMS *Ajax* after the River Plate action. (J&C McCutcheon Collection)

A day after the *Doric Star*'s loss came another final signal, this time from the *Tairoa*, to the west of where the previous attack had been. The raider now seemed to be heading south-west, possibly to meet up with German cargo ships departing for home. Vice Admiral Wells, in charge of Force K, agreed with Harwood that her most likely location would be off the River Plate. Even so, on the 8th, Harwood ordered *Exeter* to patrol around the Falklands, just in case the Germans were planning a comeback to mark the twenty-fifth anniversary of the battle there in 1914. That would have been appropriate, especially as they had been led by Admiral Graf von Spee.

Harwood knew that after three months at sea, even if they were being resupplied, the raider(s) would have to make for home at some point. Unlike the Royal Navy, the Kriegsmarine did not have a network of bases and dockyards around the world. His feeling was that wherever they were, they would not resist making a final killing among the grain and wheat cargoes off the east coast of South America.

On the 12th *Exeter* rejoined the rest of the squadron. That night her gunnery officer, Lieutenant Commander Richard Jennings, had the middle watch, but did not turn in afterwards, knowing that action stations were due at dawn. The ship was on its third degree of readiness when a prearranged call from a sentry sent him to the director control tower. On the way Captain F. S. Bell bluntly ordered him to open fire on 'the *Scheer*'. Langsdorff's disguises were still having their effect.

Harwood had been right. Having sunk one more ship, the *Streonshalh*, Langsdorff finally met the three cruisers early on the morning of 13 December off the mouth of the River Plate. He mistook them for destroyers and so, ignoring orders not to go for enemy warships, attacked. At the time, they were steaming in line ahead – *Achilles*, then *Ajax*, then *Exeter*.

On *Exeter*, her crew had been at action stations for an hour, stood down, then back again at the bugler's call. *Exeter*'s masthead light lit up as a challenge to the ship sighted on their port quarter. A flash in the distance gave the answer. Jennings ordered the 8-inch guns to open fire, knowing they had a range of 30,000 yards. The enemy was plain on the horizon at 20,000.

It looked like three Davids against one Goliath, but Harwood had carefully thought out his strategy. Although he was short of one cruiser, HMS *Cumberland*, currently refuelling at Port Stanley, and the other three cruisers' armament was inferior in range to that of *Graf Spee*, he was confident that he could destroy her. His plan was to attack from different directions, so offsetting her heavier fire while also giving the cruisers the chance to spot each other's fall of shot. As far as the Royal Navy was concerned, this would be the last naval battle fought by optical rangefinders, before the advent of radar on their ships, though *Ajax*'s gunnery officer would also be assisted by the ship's Fairey Seafox scouting biplane.

Exeter swung out of line, attacking straight towards the enemy from the south, while *Ajax* and *Achilles* came round to the north. Although the 6-inch salvoes from *Ajax* and *Achilles* fell dangerously close, Langsdorff identified *Exeter* as the main threat, especially after one of her first shells hit his director tower. *Graf Spee*'s fire was very accurate, one of her first shells passing through B turret's ammunition embarkation hatch, just below the turret's gunroom, then through the sickbay, knocking over the petty officer in there. It went out through the starboard side without exploding.

Two shells struck the forward part of the cruiser and a third hit her B turret as her crew loaded for their ninth broadside. Splinters from this turned her bridge into a shambles, leaving only Captain Bell and two others standing. Another struck A turret's right gun. *Exeter* was now left with most of her main armament out of action and her steering damaged. Captain Bell, hit in the legs and with his eyes full of grit, decided to fight the ship from her after conning position, just forward of Y turret. The transmitting station, from which Jennings controlled the main armament, was out of action as well, its crew being ordered to join the damage-control parties.

For three years this crew had practised action stations every Friday. Now this paid off – they were surprisingly calm and knew what to do. The cruiser's survival was later attributed to good construction and the rapport her crew had developed with one another. Jennings left the tower and was surprised to find the compass platform abandoned. With only Y turret left in action, he put it into local control, standing on top to help with spotting.

Exeter had lost five officers and fifty-six men in ten minutes. A shell exploding just above the 4-inch magazine not only killed everyone there, but started a fire that destroyed all communications. Orders were now passed by a chain of men taken from areas where they were no longer needed, the sailmaker being at the wheel and steering on his own initiative when no orders came.

For spotting and communication purposes, *Exeter* carried a Walrus amphibian on a catapult. As this aircraft had been gashed by shrapnel and was leaking fuel, it was hastily ditched. This had to be done while other fires raged, although during a lull in the action these were brought under control. Disregarding his own safety, Jennings yelled orders from the top of Y turret down into the front of it. The crew fired ninety-five salvoes before being forced to stop by flooding.

By now those still alive included 120 wounded. Clearing debris brought bodies to light. Realising the state *Exeter* was in, Harwood ordered Bell to withdraw to Port Stanley. Bell said to the ship's doctor, when both of them drew breath, that he had been prepared to ram the enemy. Many of the surviving crew members were only in their early twenties. Their spirit was shown by the feeling that they had not done enough and were ready for more. The rum that appeared at lunchtime was very welcome. Their dead shipmates were buried at sea that afternoon, with full naval honours. The wounded were well cared for by the Falklanders.

Making a smokescreen, then dodging in and out of it to fire 6-inch broadsides, the other cruisers harried *Graf Spee*, hitting her amidships. *Achilles* took a direct hit near her bridge and *Ajax* lost the use of her after turrets after a 28-cm hit. She lost seven men and *Achilles* four. The cruisers now stood off, intending to close in later for a night torpedo attack.

Harwood commented, 'We might as well bombard the beast with snowballs,' but Langsdorff's crew had suffered as well. His ship had taken nineteen hits in all, two of them from *Exeter*'s 8-inch armament. Although *Graf Spee*'s safety was not endangered, her water desalination plants and galleys had been destroyed, there was a gash in her bows, her oil purification plant had been wrecked and her seaplane burnt out on its catapult. Thirty-six of her crew were dead, with another fifty-six wounded. Still exchanging the occasional salvo with his remaining adversaries, Langsdorff headed for the port of Montevideo in neutral Uruguay for repairs, while *Ajax* and *Achilles* waited out in the Plate estuary.

Captain Henry McCall, the British Naval Attaché, sailed with an intelligence officer around *Graf Spee*, and was surprised that she had docked there. Apart from the hole in her bows, he could see no other obvious damage.

Langsdorff was in an unenviable position. His ship had emerged from the shadows into an unwelcome spotlight. Under international law *Graf Spee* could only remain in the harbour for 72 hours. Any longer would mean internment and Uruguay was friendly with Britain. Their agents would be all over his ship in no time. It was a long way home from here and all of his main armament's ammunition had been fired. Disobeying orders to attack enemy warships had led to this, and even if he returned to Germany alive he might face a court martial. If he found the *Altmark* again and stopped to replenish from her, the British could catch up with him while he did so. Should he successfully break out, the cruisers would continue to shadow him until more powerful reinforcements arrived.

Or were they here now? Diplomatic activity in Montevideo was intense. British agents observing the new arrival were astonished to see twenty-three officer prisoners come up from below deck to be freed, again as international law demanded. They had lain below, with mixed feelings, while the fight continued above, but had suffered no casualties. Langsdorff's final words to Captain Dove, formerly of the *Africa Shell*, were, 'Your cruisers made a very gallant fight. When people fight like that, all personal enmity is lost. Those British are hard.'

When the alarm had sounded, Captain Dove had commented, 'She's come up against something bigger this time.' *Trevanion*'s captain had replied, 'I hope it's the *Renown*. She could blow this tin can out of the water!' Fortunately for them, it had not happened – so far. Force K was a long way off and low on fuel. *Ark Royal* docked at Rio de Janeiro and

Graf Spee in Montevideo harbour with sightseers in smaller ships around her. Her camouflage included a false bow wave. The ship in the background may be the German freighter *Tacoma*, which was to play a part in her scuttling. (J&C McCutcheon Collection)

Captain Hans Langsdorff amid the crowds in Montevideo. (IWM Neg. No. HU102739)

the local British Embassy staff encouraged the press to photograph her. Rio was 1,000 miles away and it would take Force K 36 hours to reach the Plate.

Realising this, Langsdorff told the Uruguayans he would leave the following day. The German Ambassador protested to them that two weeks of repairs could not possibly be completed in three days, but to no avail. His eccentric British opposite number, Eugen Millington-Drake, was enjoying this excursion into a cloak-and-dagger world and recruited the ex-prisoners to spy. Why not? Everyone else seemed to be at it. He invoked the 24-hour law, whereby, if a British ship left the harbour, *Graf Spee* could not depart in pursuit until a day had passed. In an effort to keep Langsdorff where he was, Millington-Drake sent out British ships one by one, until the exasperated Uruguayans forbade it. McCall then deliberately made a phone conversation on an insecure line, supposedly to order fuel for *Ark Royal* in Buenos Aires. Knowing how leaky communications between these two cities were, this was bound to stampede the Germans into action.

They took the bait, one man climbing *Graf Spee*'s director tower to report that he could see other British warships out there. There was only one more – *Cumberland*'s captain had anticipated events by quickly steaming from the Falklands. Convinced escape was impossible, Langsdorff signalled Berlin:

Strategic position off Montevideo. Beside the cruisers and destroyers *Ark Royal* and *Renown*. Close blockade at night; escape into open waters and breakthrough to home waters is hopeless. Request decision on whether the ship should be scuttled in spite of insufficient depth of water in estuary of Plate or whether internment is preferred.

Berlin rejected internment.

From Harwood's point of view, Langdorff might escape again. The estuary had many channels and even with *Ajax*'s Seafox overhead he could not cover them all. There was also the prospect of what would happen if *Graf Spee* came straight at him. A sudden promotion from Commodore to Rear Admiral Sir Henry Harwood KCB had been welcome, but so would an end to this awkward situation.

Langsdorff had visited his ship's sickbay – which one officer had described as 'running with blood' – and it had made a deep impression on him. With no wish to risk the lives of his remaining 1,200 crew, there was only one solution. Langsdorff took his dead ashore and buried them, with the ex-prisoners willingly attending – a mark of the esteem in which he was held by them. Early on the evening of 17 December *Graf Spee* steamed out of the harbour, watched by crowds of people. She turned west, facing upriver, then stopped her engines. An Argentinian tug evacuated the crew to a German freighter, the *Tacoma*. Just before nine o'clock that evening, smoke and flames billowed forth as scuttling charges went off.

Graf Spee on fire in the Plate estuary after her scuttling charges had exploded. (IWM Neg. No. A000006)

Above and below: Two close-ups of *Graf Spee* on fire. Just visible at the top of the director tower, forward of the main mast, is the *Seetakt* radar that Bainbridge-Bell climbed up to examine. (J&C McCutcheon Collection)

Her Wagnerian exit did not mean an end to the intrigue, for press photographs showed an unusual aerial array above her optical rangefinder. Mr L. Bainbridge-Bell, a former RAF officer turned scientist, was sent to Montevideo. Bainbridge-Bell had worked with Robert Watson-Watt's team on the development of radar at Bawdsey in East Anglia, so if anyone knew what to look for, he did. He has been described as looking like the archetypal mad scientist, with snowy hair and half-masted trousers. Be that as it may, at no small risk to himself he boarded the listing wreck and climbed the superstructure. His report stated that the ship carried radar, probably for gun-laying and working on either 57 or 114 centimetres.

Examination of pre-war shots showed that other large German warships had carried radar, which came as a surprise to British Intelligence; Royal Navy vessels would not receive it until 1941. However, someone pigeonholed this report, which did not reach the Air Ministry's Scientific Intelligence Section for another eighteen months.

Langsdorff appeared relaxed when addressing his men on the 19th, telling them they would be looked after. All but six would return to Germany. To one of his officers he said, 'Say hello to Germany for me. Say hello to my family.' Evidently the British deception had held, for in his final letter to them he described his opponents as 'overwhelmingly superior'. His daughter Inge kept that letter for sixty-six years, not revealing it until a BBC 2 *Timewatch* programme in 2006.

With the air of a man putting his affairs in order and concerned that his family should not suffer, Langsdorff wrote to the German Ambassador in Buenos Aires:

> With the ammunition remaining an attempt to break out to open and deep water was bound to fail. And yet in deep water only could I have scuttled the ship after having used up the remaining ammunition, so preventing her from falling into the hands of the enemy.
>
> I alone bear the responsibility for scuttling *Graf Spee*. I am happy to pay with my life to prevent any possible reflection on the honour of the flag. I shall meet my fate with firm faith in the cause of the nation and of the Führer.

In the early hours of 20 December Langsdorff lay down on a flag in a room at the Buenos Aires Naval Arsenal and shot himself. It was not a swastika flag, but that of the Imperial German Navy, and perhaps an indication of his final attitude to the Nazi regime. The ex-prisoners were represented at his funeral by Captain Pottinger of the *Ashlea*.

Gradually *Graf Spee* sank into the estuary. A proposal after the war by a West German businessman to salvage her came to nothing. Her remains are still visible from the air.

✳   ✳   ✳

Above and below: The funeral of the *Graf Spee*'s crewmen at Montevideo, attended by their former prisoners. (J&C McCutcheon Collection)

There was one loose end from this affair – or rather, 293 of them – the prisoners crammed onto the tanker *Altmark*, which was still in the South Atlantic.

Launched in 1937 specifically as a supply ship for commerce raiders, the *Altmark* had left Germany on 6 August – a fortnight before *Graf Spee* – loaded a cargo of diesel in Texas and then made her first rendezvous on 1 September. Having disguised herself as the Norwegian *Sogne*, she spent the next three months in the South Atlantic, replenishing *Graf Spee*'s stocks of food, fuel and ammunition. In return she received the prisoners, 7 officers with 286 men, in basic accommodation as this use had not been foreseen. They were housed in 'flats' – holds that lacked washing facilities, proper ventilation or sanitary conditions.

The *Altmark* at Jossingfjord on 16 February 1940. (IWM Neg. No. HU27803)

Like the rest of the world, her crew listened to a radio account of the scuttling. Once that was over, there arose a new concern for their own fate. They were thousands of miles from home, with enemy warships that had been sailing for the Plate now looking for them.

However, Captain Heinrich Dau was a resourceful skipper. Like Langsdorff, he had served in the Imperial German Navy, before taking command of vessels of the Hamburg-Amerika and North German Lloyd Lines in the interwar years. Unlike Langsdorff, he was a staunch Nazi.

Dau appeared fearsome and fanatical to everyone on board. He spoke of his intention to blow up the *Altmark* rather than allow her to fall into enemy hands. Not content with that, he wanted revenge and, to the amazement of his fellow officers, proposed to attack the British naval base at Cape Town in South Africa. To their relief, these officers managed to convince Dau that the ship's light anti-aircraft armament was insufficient for such a purpose.

Cunning as well as irrational, Dau realised the British would expect him to head for home immediately. He therefore remained in the vastness of the South Atlantic for now, avoiding the shipping lanes and areas subject to British air reconnaissance. More disguises were tried, the *Altmark* becoming first the *Haugesund* and later the *Chiriqui*.

The prisoners, miserable in the damp and stinking holds below, plotted their own revenge. Attempts to drop messages overboard, in the hope that Allied ships would pick them up, were thwarted by watchful guards. Trying to break out and take over, they were driven back by high pressure hoses.

Finally, in January 1940 Dau headed for home, after his crew had carried out essential repairs and serviced the engines. Maintaining radio silence while scanning the airwaves for any information, they derived some comfort from improved weather conditions at the Equator, but in the North Atlantic things worsened again.

With little else to do, the prisoners continued to plot. It is not hard to imagine the arguments that occurred between those eager to escape at any cost and those who pointed out that any further attempts could lead to casualties or give Dau an excuse to add to their troubles. One idea was to inflate a contraceptive with hydrogen, attach a note and hope that some suitable recipient would find it. Another was for the strongest swimmer to raise the alarm as soon as land was sighted. Neither of those ideas went ahead.

The English Channel was clearly out of the question, so the only course home was round the north of Scotland. Characteristically, Dau proposed a quick though risky course close to the Shetlands, but his officers pointed out that a more cautious one, between Iceland and the Faroe Islands, with its poor weather and less frequent British naval patrols, gave a better chance of escaping detection. Heading east, then south, they would seek the sanctuary of Norwegian territorial waters. Off southern Norway they would be within range of their own aircraft and naval forces.

The tanker safely negotiated the Iceland–Faroes gap, but not without seeing trawlers and a frightening night encounter with an unidentified warship, whose lookouts did not spot them. By now feeling more confident, Dau ordered his crew to reinstate their ship's name and to store her guns below deck. Yes, she would be German, but was to pose as an unarmed supply ship. If she could maintain that, it was unlikely that passage would be denied. Dau was aware that, as with *Graf Spee* in Montevideo, any prisoners on board had to be released once neutral territory was reached.

As in 1914–18, Norway, a country with a strong pacifist tradition, had sought to keep out of this war. Aware that their country offered several useful ports and a route into the North Atlantic, the Norwegians had tried hard not to annoy the Germans, evidently in the naïve belief that as the Kaiser had respected their neutrality a generation before, Hitler might do the same.

Already Norway had been involved in two incidents. The previous October the *City of Flint*, one of the ships involved in the rescue of the *Athenia*'s survivors and subsequently captured by the *Deutschland*, had been interned by the Norwegians under international law. Then in November the *Westerwald*, the *Altmark*'s sister ship, had created a problem by passing through the prohibited defence zone by the Bergen naval base. Fearing further embarrassment, the Norwegian Navy had anticipated Dau's intentions, circulating an internal bulletin in January that the *Altmark* was probably heading for their waters, with British prisoners aboard.

On 14 February the *Altmark* was observed by coastguards north of Trondheim. Within an hour a Norwegian motorboat, the *Trygg*, carried out an inspection. Putting on a civil face, Dau assured the Norwegians that the *Altmark* was not armed. As a naval auxiliary vessel, she should be exempt from search. No mention was made of prisoners.

The Norwegians seemed satisfied, gave Dau a pilot and allowed him to proceed. However, despite three more inspections taking place, they still did not fully search the tanker, and noise made by the prisoners was drowned out by the sound of winches turning over on deck. Some Norwegians seemed to be walking a tightrope and seeing what they wished to see, but others became increasingly suspicious, especially when Dau refused to allow a search of his ship before it entered the Bergen defence zone.

One officer with more backbone than some of his fellow countrymen sent off a message to the Norwegian Admiralty: 'The vessel has refused additional inspection and passage through the defended area is therefore denied. Prisoners of war are likely to be aboard.'

The atmosphere was reminiscent of a First World War newspaper cartoon, in which the US president, Woodrow Wilson, had said 'Very inopportune' when faced with demands to abandon neutrality and support Britain.

By now Dau was complaining over the air to the German Legation in Oslo, Berlin was taking an interest, and the affair had all the makings of an international incident. Then the Norwegian Foreign Ministry reclassified the *Altmark* as no longer being a warship, so removing the barrier to the defence zone. Again, there was no mention of prisoners.

All this had at last shown the Royal Navy where the tanker was. Early on the morning of the 16th, Captain Philip Vian, leading the 4th Destroyer Flotilla, received a succinct signal from Admiral Forbes: '*Altmark* your objective. Act accordingly.' With the cruiser HMS *Arethusa* and five destroyers under his command, Vian was certainly capable of stopping the tanker, but he was hampered by a lack of knowledge as to what she looked like. The only available photograph was one that had appeared in the *Illustrated London News*, showing two vessels. Someone had assumed that the *Altmark* was a four-masted barque, rather than the tanker in the background.

In the days before North Sea oil was discovered, Norway's roads were few and her population moved around by sea. This gave Coastal Command's patrolling Hudsons difficulty in picking the tanker out from other vessels. Conflicting reports led Vian to split his force, sending *Arethusa* with the destroyers *Intrepid* and *Ivanhoe* north. He swept south in HMS *Cossack*, with *Nubian* and *Sikh*.

There is some confusion over who first spotted the *Altmark*, but all accounts agree that it was in the early afternoon of the 16th. *Arethusa*'s gunnery officer saw her, but so did three patrolling Hudsons of 220 Squadron from RAF Thornaby. The tanker was being escorted by two Norwegian patrol boats. *Arethusa* signalled the *Altmark* to stop, but was ignored.

HMS *Cossack*. (IWM Neg. No. FL1657)

Unable to fire because of the prisoners aboard, the destroyers tried unsuccessfully to manoeuvre the *Altmark* into the open sea. Attempts to board her by small parties in boats were equally fruitless and she dodged into Jossingfjord. Here Dau must have thought himself safe, with the entrance covered by the two Norwegian boats. The British could not attack here without violating neutral waters. His ship had led a charmed life and he had made fools of the Royal Navy. This would be a story to dine out on for years to come.

Vian withdrew for further instructions. Surprisingly, Churchill consulted the Foreign Secretary, Lord Halifax, before replying, 'Unless Norwegian torpedo-boat undertakes to convey *Altmark* to Bergen with a joint Anglo-Norwegian guard on board, and a joint escort, you should board *Altmark*, liberate the prisoners and take possession of the ship pending further instructions. If Norwegian torpedo-boat interferes, you should warn her to stand off. If she fires upon you you should not reply unless attack is serious, in which case you should defend yourself, using no more force than is necessary, and ceasing fire when she desists.'

Aware that Dau had signalled his position to Germany and that Jossingfjord was within range of Luftwaffe bases, Vian had to act fast. When a further attempt at negotiation met with another refusal, he bluntly told the Norwegians that he was going to search the *Altmark* and that he could sink the patrol boats before they could fire a shot. At last, the Norwegians stood to one side.

Forty-five men under Lieutenant Bradwell Turner assembled, armed with rifles and revolvers. It was a near-piratical form of warfare that must have appealed to them enormously – and they would have been itching to go, but their enthusiasm would have been curbed by a reminder that the prisoners were not to be harmed.

Surprise was out of the question. The fjord was over a mile long, Dau was expecting trouble, and *Cossack* stood out clearly against the snowy cliffs. However, the Germans initially thought she was Norwegian. A request for identification was answered by 'Heave to, or I start with my guns.'

Even now Dau refused to give in, starting his engines and trying to ram *Cossack*'s bow with his stern. Only a glancing blow was struck and *Cossack* approached again.

Leading from the front, Turner took a long leap aboard the *Altmark*. Petty Officer Atkins, who followed him, missed his footing and would have fallen between the two ships had he not grabbed the tanker's guard rail. Turner hauled him aboard and they secured the two ships with a hemp hawser. With Sub-Lieutenant Craven, who spoke German, Turner headed for the bridge. A revolver thrust into the ribs of Schmidt, the *Altmark*'s Third Officer, dissuaded him from stopping the takeover. Surprisingly, Dau did not resist.

Gunfire echoed back from the fjord's cliffs as some Germans tried to shoot it out. Gunner Smith went down with a bullet in the arm and seven of the *Altmark*'s crew were killed, with another five wounded. Others escaped in lifeboats, lit up by *Cossack*'s searchlights. One German trying to escape across ice fell through it, whereupon two of *Cossack*'s officers, thinking he was British, jumped into the freezing water to rescue him. He did not survive, and they were fortunate to do so. Some Germans continued to fire from the shoreline.

Turner must have known he was making history. Opening a hatch, he called, 'Are there any British down there?'

'We're all British down here.'

'Come on up. The Navy's here!'

The prisoners scrambled up, at last free of darkness and filth, into a cold, frosty night with drama all around. One grabbed a sailor's Lee-Enfield and threatened to shoot Dau, but was told, 'Don't be silly, old man. This is not for private use.' Others chivalrously shook hands with their former captors before departing. Dau and his surviving crew were relieved to find that they would not in turn be captives. Vian left them behind, so avoiding further controversy, landing his guests at Leith. 220 Squadron's Hudsons escorted the flotilla home, pointing out four floating mines en route.

Propagandists on both sides made much of the incident, Goebbels condemning it as piracy but not mentioning the prisoners. The Norwegians were furious – it is said that some even demanded the prisoners be returned to the Germans – but they would change their tune two months later.

Vian and Turner both received DSOs. Vian also received many letters, though not all were adulatory – some thought he should have been executed for not shooting Dau! Also decorated were the three cruiser skippers from the Plate, CBs being awarded to Captains Bell, Parry and Woodhouse. Six DSMs were awarded to various crew members.

In February 1940 the crews of *Ajax* and *Exeter* reached home, marched through London to a heroes' welcome on the 23rd and were greeted by Churchill during luncheon at the Guildhall. As would be expected, the First Lord, determined to make the most of a victory won partly by bluff, was in fine form:

I do not suppose that the bonds which unite the British Navy to the British nation, or those which join the Navy and our Mercantile Marine were ever so strong as they are today. The brunt of the war so far has fallen on the sailormen and their comrades in the Coastal Air Force, and we have already lost 3,000 lives in a hard, unrelenting struggle which goes on night and day and is going on now without a moment's respite. The brilliant sea fight which Admiral Harwood conceived, and which those who are here executed, takes its place in our naval annals, and I might add that in a dark, cold winter it warmed the cockles of the British heart. But it is not only in those few hours of deadly action, which rivet all eyes, that the strain falls upon the Navy. Far more does it fall in the weeks and months of ceaseless trial and vigilance on cold, dark, stormy seas from whose waves at any moment death and destruction may leap with sudden roar. There is the task which these men were discharging and which their comrades are discharging. There was the task from which, in a sense, this fierce action was almost a relief.

He was not the only one to feel that way. After months of groping around trying to find U-boats, and being surprised by Prien, the Navy had been reminded by this action why it had been established; it was an action fought by men who had faced up to one another on the surface instead of sneaking around below it. There were echoes of other sea fights, from Trafalgar to Jutland.

Churchill mentioned that *Achilles*, crewed by men of the Royal Navy's New Zealand Division, was receiving the same welcome at home, then went on to extol the glory of Britain's past naval heroes:

It was not for nothing that Admiral Harwood, as he instantly at full speed attacked an enemy which might have sunk any one of his ships by a single successful salvo from its heavier guns, flew Nelson's famous signal, of which neither the new occasion, nor the conduct of all ranks and ratings, nor the final result, were found unworthy.

For Churchill and for Britain, this success could not have come at a better time, especially as now there was something else to top it off with:

To the glorious tale of the action off the Plate there has recently been added an epilogue – the rescue last week by the *Cossack* and her flotilla, under the nose of the enemy and amid the tangle of one-sided neutrality, of the British captives taken from the sunken German raider. Their rescue at the very moment when these unhappy men were about to be delivered over to German bondage proves that the long arm of British sea power can be stretched out, not only for foes but also for faithful friends. And to Nelson's signal of 135 years ago, 'England expects that every man will do his duty,' there may now be added last week's no less proud reply, 'The Navy's here!'

Vian subsequently became an admiral. Turner, surprisingly, became the British Naval Attaché in Oslo after the war.

Enraged by the whole affair, Hitler took it as evidence of a British plan to dominate Scandinavia. He now ordered detailed planning for an operation that he had first considered the previous October. This was to be codenamed Operation *Weserübung* – Weser Exercise. It would result in the invasion of Denmark and Norway the following April.

7

PHONEY FOR SOME

When this bloody war is over
No more soldiering for me
When I get my civvy suit on
Oh, how happy I shall be.

Army song, to the tune of
'What a Friend We Have in Jesus'

It is said that, when the First World War ended, an unnamed general came out of his dugout, looked at the shambles around him, stuck his swagger stick under one arm and announced, 'Right, gentlemen, now that's over we can get on with some real soldiering.'

A tendency came to the fore among all too many senior officers to regard the Army as a gentlemen's club and a refuge from the world outside. Thousands of bitter and mentally scarred men headed back to civilian life, often straight to the dole. Among those still in uniform there was a strong feeling that what had happened would not recur, coupled with a desire to return to pre-war feelings and attitudes. Tanks were seen as freaks that were unlikely to be needed again. The Royal Tank Corps was seriously neglected and the Machine Gun Corps disbanded in 1922.

Neither politicians nor the Treasury would agree to new and expensive equipment. Who was there to fight now? Germany was on her knees, crippled by internal strife and inflation. The Russians were too busy killing each other. For now, Japan was still seen as an ally. There was animosity emanating from America, resentful at British dominance of the seas, but nobody was going to re-enact Bunker Hill.

The Army's remaining units were needed to police the Empire, with additional responsibilities now that, after 1918, whole areas of the Middle East had emerged from Turkish rule. The League of Nations had given the mandate to govern Iraq, Jordan and Palestine to Britain, all of which would prove to be thankless tasks, stirring up more trouble for the future.

Like a dying steed, the horse lobby continued to kick out. Some officers believed cavalry still had a role as mounted infantry. They pointed out the lorry's limited cross-country ability, considering the tank and armoured car to be inferior and less mobile in reconnaissance. Others felt that infantry regiments would go if mechanisation continued. There was a reluctance to experiment when money was tight, and MPs fretted about those regiments that recruited in their constituencies. In 1927 Brigadier General Stewart-Vyse penned a now notorious lecture, in which he dwelt pompously on the 'lack of tradition' of the Tank Corps while extolling the virtues of 'that comparatively swift animal, the horse'. It came as no surprise to read that he was the former Inspector General of Cavalry.

Lest anyone be tempted to view this as an example of the British Army preparing for the last war and not the next one, it should be said that the British were not alone in their views. Horses were used by the Germans on a large scale up to 1945 – many of them bought from Britain in the 1930s. Even in America, where four wheels apparently reigned supreme, there was still a horsed cavalry division until 1944, the sabre being carried until ten years before.

However, changes were coming. In 1928 Churchill, then Chancellor of the Exchequer, said that the cavalry must be forced to mechanise or disband. It did not happen quickly, though in 1934 the 1st Tank Brigade became Britain's first permanent armoured formation, while senior officers worried about the morale of the remaining cavalry units. Those who had considered themselves gentlemen on horseback would have to become grubby-fingered mechanics, just like everyone else, and the troop officer would be expected to take off his coat to lend a hand as well, if needed. British armoured tactics were carefully noted by the rearming Germans. Hitler was taking a personal interest in tanks and in those who supported them.

Investment was being increased, but spread across all three Services. Stanley Baldwin's phrase 'The bomber will always get through' ensured that much of the money would go to the RAF. During 1936–37 the rest of the cavalry was ordered to mechanise, though they kept their titles. Two years later they would merge with armoured units under the umbrella title of the Royal Armoured Corps, the RTC becoming the Royal Tank Regiment.

During the interwar period the Carden-Lloyd company had experimented with a variety of small tracked armoured vehicles, resulting in three known as the Bren Carrier, the Scout Carrier and the Cavalry Carrier. It would eventually dawn on the official mind that what was needed was a standardised design, resulting in the Universal Carrier of 1940. From 1938 the infantry were reorganised, with ten carriers to each battalion. Mortar platoons, using the 3-inch variety, were added as supporting firepower. This was an improvement, and by 1939 Britain led the way in mechanisation, but there were still only enough vehicles to equip one brigade at a time, leaving the other two in an infantry division to march.

It was now realised that a new British Expeditionary Force would be needed, although the title had a tentative, reluctant feel about it. Memories of 1914–18 were still strong, and the thought of being dragged into some new French bog was not appealing. The Territorial Army was to be doubled in size and reorganised into twelve infantry divisions, three to be motorised, with one armoured division.

The changing of the guard. Khaki service dress for the Irish Guards at Buckingham Palace on 1 September 1939. (IWM Neg. No. HU55552)

Where was all this extra manpower to come from? Leslie Hore-Belisha, a politician so far best known for introducing the driving test and the famous crossing beacon, was now the Secretary of State for War. An ardent self-publicist, Hore-Belisha thought he knew more about military matters than the professionals, whose attitudes he considered outdated. Some of his measures, such as new barracks, improved pay and the chance for more men to be commissioned from the ranks, were steps in the right direction, but the way he went about this caused resentment.

War was coming nearer and volunteers would not be enough. Conscription was an alien process in Britain, and one that had only been introduced in 1916 after Kitchener's poster had pointed an accusing finger for two years. Against opposition from the Labour and Liberal parties, the Military Training Bill went through in April 1939, strongly supported by Hore-Belisha. Men of twenty to twenty-two were now liable for six months of service. They were to be known as Militiamen, and it was thought – or rather hoped – that they would mainly be employed in air defence.

This was followed on 3 September by the National Service (Armed Forces) Act, making all men between eighteen and forty-one liable for conscription. They were called up by years, the youngest first and single men before married ones. Their length of service would be 'the duration of hostilities' or 'so long as His Majesty may require'. They could state a Service preference and their regiment or corps if volunteering for the Army. In October 1939 200,000 registered. With past trench warfare in mind, it was not surprising that half volunteered for the RAF or the Navy, but, as the Army needed the most manpower, many were disappointed.

Recognition that this was going to be a technical war, and that civilians would have as much to contribute as soldiers, meant that those already in what were now termed Reserved Occupations were exempt from call-up. Examples were dockyard workers, firemen, police officers and those employed in the aviation industry. There was a medical check first, dividing recruits into categories. Category III meant fit only for limited duties – known to old sweats as 'excused breathing'. Category IV was a complete rejection. Full control of industry did not come until the middle of 1940, so, despite the urgency of the situation, at the beginning of that year a million people were still out of work.

Life changed for Army recruits as quickly as if they had been sent to another planet. Forget civilian clothes, your mother's cooking, the girl you left behind and your father's stories of life on the Somme. Soldiering was something from which you did not go home at five o'clock. Life was coarse battledress, coarse blankets and even coarser language. Life was the fire picquet, banging his pickaxe handle on the nearest locker and shouting 'Wakey, wakey!' at 6.30 in the morning.

Life was a bevy of NCOs, whose attitudes varied from the fatherly to the frightening. 'Don't think that you have got no friends, because you have. We've a load of officers who have nothing else to do all day but be your friends. So if you feel upset, go and moan to them – and a fat lot of good it will do you!'

Some of those who now wore three stripes had started life as Barnardo's boys – the Services always took a quota of them – and for them the Army was the only home they had ever known. They looked down on the new battledress, compared it to a mechanic's overalls, with no buttons to polish, and lamented the resulting low standard of turnout. The high collar made recruits feel like convicts and the baggy appearance – copied from pre-war ski clothing – made all too many look like walking sacks of potatoes. For a tall, slim man, with some assistance from the regimental tailor, it was possible to achieve a reasonably smart appearance, with comfort added by shaving the material on the inside of the trouser legs. For shorter, heavier men this was seldom possible, and in addition battledress treated with an anti-gas chemical smelt like a dead camel. Not something to impress the girls with.

Life was languid officers who spoke in condescending tones while saluting with swagger canes. Life was blancoing webbing to the required shade, then (contrary to regulations) polishing the numberless brass tags that went with it – and woe betide you should you miss one. Life was a

Nissen hut, with a concrete floor, iron bedsteads and a coke stove. Life was standing ramrod straight, with your thumbs down the seams of your scratchy new trousers, answering questions succinctly in a flat monotone. Yes, sergeant, no, sergeant. No sarges here. Life was scrubbing that floor, getting fell in outside and dressing by the right, all the while wondering what this had to do with killing Hitler.

To work, then. Life was doubling round the barrack square. Life was the born leader, the former cadet who was sure to earn a stripe quickly. Life was the quiet bespectacled grammar school boy, the victim of a bullying corporal. Life was the tough slum kid with a pasty face and bad teeth who seldom spoke and had difficulty reading. Life was the Jonah.

No squad was (or is) complete without a Jonah. This character broke wind during the colonel's inspection, about turned to the left, marched right arm, right leg and, while in the sandbagged throwing bay, dropped the grenade while throwing the pin.

Life was the assault course, climbing over, under or through a variety of fiendish obstacles while some sadist fired burst after burst from one of the new Thompson guns overhead. Keep your backside down or get a second fundamental. Life was a slit trench, 2 feet wide by 6 feet long by 5 feet deep, the spoil heaped up round the edge, shared with the barrack-room drunk who, as a form of field punishment, carried the heavy Boys anti-tank rifle.

Life was guard duty on a snow-covered barrack gate – two hours on, four off, with an infantry exercise next morning. Life was moving by section, spaced 10 yards apart, up a narrow country lane while looking enviously at some fat civilian driving by in a black car. Life was having your horizons shrink to the camp, your mates, as they now were, and what you might expect tomorrow.

Life was not Thursday, Friday or Saturday. Life was the final exercise day, field-firing day and passing-out day – the day when even the Jonah realised he had achieved something.

Next came trade training. For the infantry, it meant more of the above, with tall moustachioed sergeants, newly returned from anti-terrorist duties in Palestine, saying, 'They're gutless, those depot bestards. You don't find them where the action is.' For the signallers, it meant telling dashes from dots, then scrambling up telegraph poles to wrestle with cables. For the sappers, it meant digging culverts, handling explosives, building pontoon bridges, laying mines and – later – bomb disposal. For tank crews, it meant wielding spanners on obsolete Vickers vehicles and, when the new Matildas arrived, carefully passing 2-pounder shells through a narrow open hatch. For the mechanics, who had often followed this trade at civilian garages, it meant new vehicles, from Bedford 15-hundredweights to Bren carriers.

The infantry, long accustomed to the trusty Lee-Enfield rifle, had from 1937 been issued with the accurate and reliable Bren light machine gun. Then there was the Vickers medium machine gun, another 1914–18 relic, heavy to carry but capable, with new improved ammunition, of firing up to 3,500 yards. The Thompson gun, which the War Office had once looked down on as a gangster's weapon, was now coming on the scene, and the few who had them were envied by their mates, but further supplies would have to reach Britain via the North Atlantic and its U-boats.

There was a lack of everything. Due to a battledress shortage some units went to France looking much as their fathers had done, with the new webbing but in the old khaki service dress. The Royal Artillery crossed over with a ragbag of old and newer weapons, the 25-pounders now coming into service being initially modified from the older 18-pounder. The 2-pounder, with the promise of a 6-pounder to follow, equipped the anti-tank units.

Signals equipment was in short supply and often did not extend beyond tank troop leader level. Nor were tank radios always compatible with infantry ones. For a country that had invented the tank, Britain was showing extraordinary weakness. None of the variety of vehicles the BEF fielded mounted anything bigger than a 2-pounder, and the Matilda Mark I lacked even that, carrying only a machine gun. Not only that, but the 2-pounder shell had been designed with British-made armour in mind. It was homogenous – the same thickness all the way through – as opposed to German armour, which was face-hardened. No one knew it yet, but in the battles to come 2-pounder shot would frequently hit accurately, then shatter without penetrating. The Boys anti-tank rifle would turn out to be all but useless and become quickly outdated.

So much for the weapons and the conditions of service. What of the country they were going to? Most of the BEF's troops had never been abroad, and as their ships approached the French docks they would have felt a mixture of curiosity and apprehension. Then it was time to shoulder packs and march off through pleasant if unremarkable countryside to a transit camp, somewhere in the middle of nowhere.

In 1914 Kaiser Wilhelm II had – allegedly – referred to their fathers as 'that contemptible little army', although its subsequent performance at Mons must have given him pause for thought. Now things seemed to be repeating themselves. Here they were again, with many of the same weapons and – what was worse – the same ideas, including an expectation by some of those who commanded them that they would be able to pick up where they had left off in 1918. It was a world of straight roads flanked by poplar trees, hastily erected huts, cobbled streets and estaminets that had quickly added egg and chips to the menu. Those who could remember their schoolboy French now found it came in handy. The situation was summed up by the ukulele player George Formby when he came to entertain them:

Now imagine me in the Maginot Line
Sitting on a mine in the Maginot Line

The BEF disembarking in September 1939. (IWM Neg. No. o-000011)

> Now it's turned out nice again
> The Army life is fine
> French girls make a fuss of me
> I'm not French as you can see
> But I know what they mean when they say, 'Oui, Oui'
> Down on the Maginot Line.

As to future combat:

> Hitler can't hit us a lot
> His secret weapon's tommyrot
> You ought to see what the sergeant's got
> Down on the Maginot Line.

Apart from Poland, Hitler at present seemed disinclined to hit anyone. Newsreel cameras showed soldiers in sports kit panting in threes as they ran along the roads, or wrestling to assemble 3-inch mortars amid the local agriculture. Chamberlain showed his face too, although his speech was halting and indecisive, reflecting his feelings at the time. He would have given anything to get off this hook, but there seemed no escape.

What of the Maginot Line? France had spent a fortune on it in the 1930s, building a chain of forts from the Swiss frontier along the German one. Its soldiers' cap badges bore the motto '*On Ne Passe Pas*'. Indeed, as at Verdun, the Germans would not pass here. Its massive blockhouses with their characteristic French curves in concrete, its mortars and machine guns protected by embrasures or by mushroom-like domes that rose magically out of the ground, the belts of barbed wire and railway lines planted deeply into the ground on its eastern side as tank traps – all this was a formidable and well-designed obstacle.

Beneath the man-made hills over half a million French soldiers waited, in a strange Jules Verne-like world. This was a mixture of the old and the new – a throwback to living in caves, but with every modern convenience. There were dormitories, hospitals, kitchens, cinemas, sun-ray rooms to counter the lack of natural sunlight, gas-proof doors and even a narrow-gauge underground electric railway to speed troops along from the entrances on the Line's western side. The one at Hackenberg fort is open to the public today at weekends. Travelling on it is a short but noisy experience, not quickly forgotten. Everything from accommodation to ammunition magazines was protected by several feet of solid earth – the earth they were determined no German would set foot on again.

In spite of all this, living in the forts was a damp and dreary experience. Bunks were stacked up to five tiers high, and those unfortunate enough to occupy the top ones had difficulty in getting under the blankets without banging their heads on the roof. Their superiors tried to counter this as far as possible by housing men in barracks on the surface behind the forts. They could be quickly sent below again when needed.

The Line ran through Alsace-Lorraine – a disputed territory that had changed hands twice since 1870. The towns and villages within it had German-sounding names, reflecting its past history, and a population whose sympathies were not all with the Third Republic. Also, although it had never been intended to be a secret, the Germans knew a good deal more about it than the Allies would have liked. During construction a variety of firms had been involved, including some German ones that had put in low tenders. There was no better way of learning about such a structure than from those who had helped to build it.

During the autumn of 1939 and the following spring the Line would see a variety of high-ranking visitors. These included Lord Gort, the BEF's Commander-in-Chief, King George VI and the Duke of Windsor, the latter given back a form of respectability with the uniform of a major general.

Among them was Lieutenant General Sir Alan Brooke, one of the BEF's corps commanders. After his first visit in 1939 he wrote in his diary:

> The whole conception of the Maginot Line is a stroke of genius. And yet! It gives me but little feeling of security and I consider that the French would have done better to invest the money in the shape of mobile defences such as more and better aircraft and more heavy armoured divisions rather than sink all this money into the ground.

A second visit early the following year did not make him feel any better:

A false sense of security is engendered, of sitting behind an impregnable iron fence; and should the fence perchance be broken, the French fighting spirit might well be brought crumbling with it.

He was not the only one to feel that way. The French had forgotten Napoleon Bonaparte's saying that the side that stays within its fortifications is beaten. In any case, they did not go far enough. The Line had not been extended along the Belgian border, in case the Belgians should think France was going to desert them. They and the Dutch had opted for neutrality, hoping that it would be respected this time.

The BEF's few divisions were indeed worthy of German contempt, and that of the French, who considered 'perfidious Albion' was not taking this war seriously. Clearly the BEF was not going to attack, but there was no will in France to go forward either. The only offensive the French mounted was a brief foray into the Saar, occupying a few small hamlets that the Germans had willingly given up. Realising this had done nothing to relieve the pressure on the Poles, they fired a few shots, were filmed by the newsreel cameras, giving new meaning to 'the watch on the Rhine', then returned without having achieved anything.

Some French units were well turned out, but all too many were scruffy and surly in their manner. Paraded before senior officers and ordered to give an 'Eyes right!' when passing them, not every man did so. Clearly, the *poilu* of 1939 was not the man his father had been. In 1914 the cry had been 'On to Berlin!' This time it was a resigned 'Let's get it over with.'

A too-rapid mobilisation of skilled men had disrupted French industry, taking weeks to sort out. Conditions of service were poor, leave hard to come by and often used to make money on the side. 'French leave' became a fact of life, with men slipping away from their units at weekends, returning the following Monday. Drunkenness was rife and French railway stations set aside a room for drying out men before putting them on the returning trains.

Few war films ever convey the sheer tedium of the soldier's lot. There is an old British Army saying that war is 99 per cent boredom and 1 per cent fright. Having settled into huts or tents – then wondering how long before the next move – the BEF's life consisted of parades, guard duties, fire picquets and stacking an endless flood of supplies in dumps. Everything was on the move and had to be accounted for, from hut chimneys to pickaxes, stowed beneath trees or out in the open under camouflage netting. Some troops were employed on airfield construction, turning the RAF's new fields into something more civilised.

As a gesture of support to their French allies, and to gain experience under operational conditions, infantry battalions were ordered, in rotation, into the Saar front line. Life for those involved shrank to the trenches they had dug, as much to keep warm as for any defensive purpose. Their horizon was the next field, the hedge bordering it and the dark wood in the distance, and all the while they wondered what the enemy was like, whether the stories old soldiers had told them were true, and if they were under observation.

For those with old campaign ribbons on new battledress the world seemed to have come full circle. Here they were again, shovels in hand, squinting through gunsights, waiting for something to happen while hoping it would wait until they came off duty. A photo taken in the British front line during the winter of 1939/40 shows a trench leading into a dugout, manned by steel-helmeted men in greatcoats. Only the Bren on its sustained-fire tripod gives any indication that this scene did not date from a generation before.

When the time could be spared, parties of soldiers visited the 1914–18 cemeteries. These poignant reminders of a previous generation, with neat rows of pale grey headstones around a Cross of Sacrifice, were immaculately maintained by the gardeners of what was then the Imperial War Graves Commission, some of whom were former British soldiers who had stayed behind and married local French girls. Now middle-aged, these were men whose youth had come to an end in the chalky trenches of the Somme or the mud of Passchendaele. They had been as much casualties of that conflict as those whose graves they now tended.

Remembrance Day in 1939 took on a new meaning. Many men standing in the ranks that November day would have had only one thought in mind: how long before it's our turn? For some it was worse when they came across the grave of the father they had never known.

Then there were the German graves – sombre black crosses in the soil of a country they had failed to conquer. Now it was all set to start again. So much for a war to end wars.

It was not long before the graves were added to. On 9 December Corporal Thomas Priday of the King's Shropshire Light Infantry became the BEF's first fatal casualty when he trod on a French mine, wounding six other troops. He was twenty-seven. His funeral at Luttange Communal Cemetery was an elaborate affair, attended by a French honour guard and the local corps commander.

Whatever his nationality, it was easy for a soldier occupying a muddy trench in the autumn raid to question why he was there, especially as nothing seemed to be happening. The French Communist Party, urged on by Moscow's friendship with Hitler, engaged in acts of sabotage. The phrase '*Pour Qui Et Pour Quoi?*', daubed on walls in red, accompanied by a hammer and sickle, summed up their feelings. For who and for what?

Encouraged by German propaganda, the *poilus* envied the larger amounts that British soldiers were paid – 17 francs a day for them, 50 centimes a day for the French – and suspected the Tommies were set up well behind the lines in some cosy billet, making free with their women. These were the same comments the British would later make about the Americans.

In an attempt to make up for the Maginot Line's deficiencies, new efforts were made to extend it northwards, though the additions were inevitably of inferior quality. Across the frontier the Germans were adding to what they called the Westwall. While this went on, the American correspondent William L. Shirer noted that each side worked in full view of the other without a shot being fired. 'A queer kind of war,' he observed.

Handling shovels more often than rifles, the BEF dug anti-tank ditches and put in pillboxes along the Belgian frontier. Much of this was carried out in the coldest winter for fifty years, freezing the Channel at Boulogne. Wags said that this force's initials stood for 'Back Every Friday', but those who did get Christmas leave found themselves crowded onto grubby trains steaming into London's Victoria station, where a chalked sign warned them which train to catch, and when, on return.

Getting back to your mother's cooking, and actually sleeping between sheets for once, would have been welcome, but the time away was short and everyone knew the penalty for overstaying. Girls they had known now said 'Oh, it's doing you good' when confronted by slimmer, fitter and stronger men. Down the pub old soldiers wanted to swap tales while hearing new ones. Mons was fought all over again and uniform had to be worn off duty. Anyone changing into civilian clothes risked finding a white feather in his coat pocket when he headed home. It was a First World War symbol of cowardice that was making an unwelcome comeback.

Some units celebrated Christmas where they stood. The Norfolk Regiment's 2nd Battalion had been shipped to France the previous September, digging trenches and in December meeting an assortment of VIPs ranging from the King to Churchill. On Christmas Eve, accompanying the rest of the 4th Brigade, they were ordered south, their final move from the town of Metz being in conditions of minus 22 degrees Centigrade. For the Norfolks the festive season turned out to be a nightmare as the anti-freeze in their vehicles froze. After five difficult days and nights they reached the front line, taking over from the grateful men of the Black Watch's 1st Battalion.

Home now would be the Saar, scene of skirmishes between the French and Germans since the short-lived offensive three months before. On New Year's Day the Norfolks were in the *ligne de contact*. Behind them was the Maginot Line and in front No Man's Land – an area of French territory that the Germans had taken over. The enemy was now about half a mile away, in undulating countryside made up of fields and clumps of woodland.

Establishing their headquarters in the village of Waldweisstroff, the Norfolks showed keenness by ringing the church bells in a small hamlet. This caused consternation among the French but, to the newcomers' disappointment, the enemy did not react.

On the evening of the 4th they sent out two patrols, one led by Lieutenant Patrick Everitt and the other by Captain Francis Barclay, the A Company commander. Lightly equipped, with leather jerkins over their battledress to give some extra warmth, Everitt's men headed north-west, crossing thick

French-laid wire with difficulty to a stream, which they forded, passing through the German lines but seeing no one.

The tension can be imagined. At night sound matters more than sight, carrying well across open ground. Movement has to be slow, with frequent listening halts. Patrolling can be a nerve-wracking experience, with the feeling that the enemy is all around you, ready to strike while remaining invisible. A tuft of gorse becomes a crouching man, and wind in a forest, waving branches and creaking trees, sounds like a phantom army. In addition, dark uniforms would have shown up clearly against the white fields.

Now over the German border, Everitt's patrol crossed a road running parallel to it, halting near a small wood. Still there was no sign of the enemy, and after cutting some telephone lines as a gesture they returned shortly before midnight. Their brigadier congratulated them on a notable first for the Norfolks.

Barclay's patrol, which included Second Lieutenant Murray Brown and three men, had left an hour earlier. Passing through Lohmuhl Wood, they headed towards a railway line that ran into the village of Waldwisse. Barclay's orders were to gather information on the German positions behind barbed wire near the station and, if possible, a prisoner.

They found a way through the wire and crossed the line. Ahead fresh boot prints followed a clear path to a house. Smoke was coming from the chimney, but everything was quiet. With Murray Brown and two men outside as a covering party, Barclay and Lance Corporal Davis moved forward, their hope of an easy capture being dashed when they found the house empty. Leaving Murray Brown in a covering position to the south-east, Barclay led the rest of the patrol to investigate an outhouse and a bridge over a stream. The outhouse also proved to be empty and the bridge had been wired underneath. A return to the house showed it still to be empty.

Then a grenade exploded behind the patrol, causing them to run to the east side of the road, using a ditch as cover. With his binoculars, Barclay checked the ground ahead for Murray Brown, but could see no sign of him. He threw a grenade into the house's archway but restrained his men from firing for fear of hitting his fellow officer.

Now all hell broke loose, grenades mixed with gunfire coming from ahead and to either side. Rather than be surrounded, the patrol ran back a further 50 yards. There was still no sign of the missing officer. They moved quickly across the road and railway, but any hope of circling to the right in search of Murray Brown was dashed as flares illuminated the dark sky.

As they were outnumbered withdrawal was the only course. Despite the volume of fire, no one was hit and they returned safely to battalion headquarters. Barclay had taken his second-in-command on patrol without his CO's permission, for which the brigadier took him to task. It was fortunate for him that Murray Brown returned unharmed.

Having become separated from the rest of the covering party, Murray Brown had made his way to the railway line, to hear two men talking on top of a bridge. That ceased when he threw a grenade. One man moved as if to cut him off – Murray Brown fired a rifle shot at him and went to see if he had been hit but could not find him. A Very light came up from the house and grenades were thrown at him as he lay in the snow, but they did no harm.

Heart thumping, Murray Brown moved back to the railway line, then listened for 15 minutes, trying to locate the rest of the patrol. All he heard were mortar bombs exploding near the stream. Guessing the others had got away, he waited a further half-hour, then headed back.

His adventures were not yet over. Trying to locate A Company's position, he turned right too soon and was fired on again, this time by the French. He lay low until daybreak, then moved off in the right direction, arriving safely despite the efforts of French snipers. With his return, the patrol was deemed a success, with praise now for Barclay, whose brigadier reckoned it to be 'the best bit of news that's happened since the BEF came out here'. To Barclay's further surprise, he received the Military Cross and Lance Corporal Davis the Military Medal. Murray Brown and the other two members, Lance Corporals Harris and Spooner, were all Mentioned in Despatches. These were the first awards given to the BEF.

However, the Norfolks would soon gain another and more dubious distinction. On the morning of 7 January, as the rest of the battalion moved out of the line, Lieutenant Everitt's carrier platoon remained as part of the brigade's 'patrol team'. This time he and ten men were to cover a working party of twenty men from the Border Regiment's 1st Battalion, tasked with laying wire in front of Lohmuhl Wood.

At midday, Everitt, armed with a pistol, led the patrol off in mist over snowy ground towards the crest of a hill. They stopped on reaching the top and could plainly see Germans moving round, apparently unaware of them. An NCO twice called to Everitt to keep down, but he, evidently scorning the danger, continued forward. Then a machine gun opened up, followed by other weapons, which sent the rest of the patrol diving for cover.

Everitt ran towards the Germans, firing as he went, and was cut down. The patrol, realising any attempt at recovery would be suicidal, pulled back, scrambling over the hill in full view of the enemy. A second patrol that night failed to locate him.

Two days later German radio announced that Everitt had died. Why he had gone over the hill and continued to advance, lightly armed, when his patrol had been required to do no more than protect the wiring party, will never be known. Aggression, impatience, a desire for recognition, perhaps, or to make up for Barclay's patrol not coming back with a prisoner. Everitt was the first BEF officer to die in action.

8

ELDERS AND BETTERS

So much for life at platoon level. What of the commanders? On the war's outbreak Lord Gort was appointed Commander-in-Chief of the BEF.

John Standish Surtees Prendergast Vereker, 6th Viscount Gort, owed his present status to Leslie Hore-Belisha's policy of clearing out what he saw as dead wood by appointing younger generals. A Grenadier Guardsman with a string of decorations including the Victoria Cross, Gort had, in December 1937, gone up two ranks to full general, becoming the youngest ever Chief of the Imperial General Staff. Gort was a soldier rather than a politician, seen as courageous, loyal and austere, being accustomed to privations, with a schoolboy sense of humour. Hore-Belisha had hoped that by putting him into the top job he would add to the drive for reform, that his character would appeal to the troops and enhance the Army's standing with the public. In so rising he had been promoted over the heads of several other senior officers, among them Generals Brooke, Dill and Wavell. Gort was a man with enemies, not all of them German.

It had been a mistake. Gort did not work well with Hore-Belisha, hating his flamboyant personality, his unorthodox appointments within the Army and his reliance on the advice of the military writer Basil Liddell Hart. For several months before the war's outbreak Gort and Hore-Belisha had seen little of each other and had barely been on speaking terms. Hore-Belisha had increasingly dealt with either Gort's deputy or other staff officers.

Gort was seen as too formal, too inclined to stick to his principles, and paying too much attention to detail while neglecting the broader picture. At a senior officers' conference, with Hore-Belisha present, Gort had asked whether a tin hat, when not worn on the head, should go on the right or left shoulder. On another occasion he had asked about the use of grenades and how many a patrol should carry. After visiting the Maginot Line Brooke had tried to discuss faults in the French outposts with Gort, who had replied, 'Oh, I have not had time to think of it yet, but look, what we must go into is the proper distribution of sandbags.' Other concerns of his had been the tearing-off ignition paper on rockets, anti-freeze mixture, and night-flying pigeons.

Gort had rightly felt that the pre-1939 plans to send only two divisions to the Continent were totally inadequate, but he had failed to press the case for mechanisation, or to form armoured divisions. He had also failed to gain much increase in the RAF's air-cooperation squadrons, or to gain BEF authority over their Advanced Air Striking Force.

Not surprisingly, when war came he had welcomed his new appointment as a chance to get away from Hore-Belisha and the War Office. On reaching the Staff College to form his headquarters, Gort had said, 'Here we go again, marching off to war. I can't expect everybody to be as thrilled as I am.' Here was a real soldier's job, even though at fifty-six he was now too old for front-line action.

Someone who was not as thrilled was General Edmund 'Tiny' Ironside – so nicknamed as he stood 6 feet 4 inches. An open-air, active soldier who had played rugby for Scotland when younger, he loathed desk work and the War Office. In 1936 he had been GOC Eastern Command, commenting in his diary, 'We are in no fit state to go to war. There are no men and there is no money for their equipment and there is no will among the Cabinet Ministers to want an Army ... We have nothing with which to fight – literally nothing – and will have nothing for the next two years.' Two years later he had felt no better. 'Never again shall we even contemplate a Force for a foreign country. Our contribution is to be the Navy and the RAF.'

Despite an anti-Semitic streak, Ironside had welcomed Hore-Belisha. 'We are at our lowest ebb in the Army and the Jew may resuscitate us ... He is ambitious and will not be as lazy as some of the others were. He starts in when things are at their worst and will have to show results.'

Moving on to Inspector General of Overseas Forces, and by now thinking that the Middle East was where the British Army's main effort would be made if war came, Ironside visited Poland in July 1939. His prophetic view was that France would not attack in the west and that Poland would be quickly occupied. Aware of the British government's muddle, he wrote, 'They are all dreamers and thinkers and cannot turn them into orders. Not a good augury for war.'

On the afternoon of 3 September Ironside had been summoned from Aldershot to become Chief of the Imperial General Staff, taking over Gort's position, instead of leading the BEF, to which he felt he was more suited. Gort, familiar with the war plans, had been removed from them just when he was most needed. Ironside, who had never served in the War Office, was ill-suited to the job. It would have been better to have appointed General Dill as the BEF C-in-C, left Gort where he was and to have made use of Ironside's French in a liaison capacity. Instead, this function went to the Duke of Gloucester – a decent man but not a particularly bright one.

For now, this suited Hore-Belisha. He had got rid of Gort and brought in Ironside, who he wrongly thought he could dominate. His scrapping of 'Buggins' Turn' had resulted in two senior officers now holding jobs for which neither was entirely fitted – a fact which he was to realise in the months to come.

Ironside made it clear to the politicians that the French would not go on the offensive. They would sit indefinitely in the Maginot Line and demand more British troops. For this they had some justification – sending just four divisions across the Channel in five weeks was not much of a commitment to the Allied cause. With his fellow chiefs, MRAF Newall and Admiral Pound, Ironside found himself caught up in an endless series of meetings. These included the War Cabinet, the Chiefs of Staff Committee, the Supreme Council of the Allies, the Military Co-ordination Committee, the Board of the Admiralty, the Army Council and the Air Council. Politics required everyone to have a say, so there was no prompt decision-making. Apart from the stalemate across the Channel, there was the question of how to defend the Empire. What of Italy and Japan – neutral for now, but for how long?

Further frustrations were caused by the attitude of the Belgians, intent on learning the wrong lessons from 1914. Their neutrality held and they would not allow any defences on their soil, thinking it more likely that the Germans would invade them again if they did. There were therefore no staff talks and no joint plans.

Ironside's diary criticisms continued:

> The old gentlemen sitting here in London have no idea of the seriousness of the position ... How can we get a unified command of operations? How are we to stop these stupid conferences of the Chiefs of Staff and War Cabinets, discussing the little details of the things that have happened?

The Cabinet's 'wait and see' policy depressed him and he saw Chamberlain as 'a weary, tired old man, dominating at all times the other mediocrities who bear the responsibility with him'.

The BEF corps commanders, Brooke and Dill, had their own problems, which Brooke, an unhappy warrior and no friend of Ironside, frequently aired in his diary. Nor were his criticisms confined to his own countrymen – he saw the French as 'disgruntled and insubordinate' after attending one of their parades.

Dill too expected to command the BEF, but after Hore-Belisha's decision said, 'I have no real complaint. I have lived long enough to know that these things have a way of righting themselves if one leaves them alone.' He also saw Hore-Belisha as too apt to meddle, and this may have affected his relations with Churchill later on.

Two of the BEF's divisional commanders were to gain fame later on, although one had acquired a certain notoriety already.

Major General Harold Alexander, formerly of the Irish Guards, with a DSO and MC from the Western Front last time round, was artistic but not intellectual, charming, blessed with no inner conflict or self-doubt, and seeing himself as a man of action. A good, common sense, regimental soldier with a steady pair of hands, he would lead the 1st Infantry Division, serving well during the Dunkirk retreat, in Burma and the Mediterranean.

Major General Bernard Montgomery, leading the 3rd Infantry Division, could hardly have been a greater contrast and saw Alexander as having no brains. Logical, tactless, abrasive, accepting no excuse for idleness, Montgomery had passed through Staff College but had regarded the curriculum as 'all nonsense'. Brooke, a fellow student at Camberley, had pulled strings to get him his present command. An austere, teetotal widower and a soldier in the Cromwellian mould, Montgomery spared no effort to make his men fit, earning his unit the nickname of 'The Iron Division'. Although the day of the black beret had yet to dawn, at a time when smart service dress, riding breeches and high-topped boots were the norm, Montgomery stood out by wearing battledress – the first senior British officer to do so and probably a deliberate choice.

The French commanders did not inspire confidence, either among many of their own troops or their British opposite numbers. General Maurice Gamelin was Chief of the General Staff of National Defence for France. A young and competent divisional commander from 1916, by now he was sixty-eight and ensconced in his headquarters, a gloomy castle at the town of Vincennes. Its main claim to fame was that Henry V had died there of dysentery.

This building has been described as being like a submarine without a periscope. Incredibly, it had no radio contact with other headquarters. There were no teleprinters either, and messages were despatched by motorcycle on the hour. When once asked how long it took a message to reach the front line, Gamelin replied that it was usually about 48 hours – a fact that did not seem to concern him. Here there was no Hore-Belisha to clear out dodos in favour of younger men. Gamelin had been in uniform for so long at so high a level that it seemed no one had the nerve to ask him to step down. An intellectual, he felt ill at ease with the troops, of whom he saw little, and Paul Reynaud, soon to become France's Prime Minister, said of him, 'He might be all right as a prefect or a bishop, but he is not a leader of men.'

Gort's four divisions, grouped into two corps, came under General Georges, commander of the Armies of the North-East. He had risen entirely through merit and was seen by many as France's best soldier. Though under Gamelin, Georges and his superior were hardly on speaking terms; and as there was doubt as to the limit of each other's responsibilities, Gamelin frequently bypassed Georges to order Gort directly, which did not help matters.

On 9 November Gamelin explained to Gort his intention to abandon the frontier defences and march into Belgium in the event of a German attack – known as Plan D. Gort was unhappy, but suppressed his feelings in the cause of Allied unity. His detractors would later see his acceptance of it as a dereliction of duty.

During this month Hore-Belisha visited the BEF. The weather was foul, and it is not hard to imagine Gort's glee at finally being given the opportunity to show this politician what a real soldier's life was like. Hore-Belisha was given a pair of fur-lined boots, which turned out not to

Generals Gort and Gamelin in October 1939. (IWM Neg. No. 0-000158)

be waterproof, then had to climb a bank while Gort explained a 1914–18 battle. When they finally reached shelter in a chateau, Gort flung open a window, letting in an icy draught while shouting 'Isn't it a grand day!' Bully beef sandwiches were provided – at least they were not pork – and when a decent meal finally came Hore-Belisha's way Gort hung around, making jocular remarks.

Hore-Belisha gritted his teeth and endured it all. He had asked to see the troops rather than the defences and therefore did not see the full picture of work completed or in progress. He made no criticisms to Gort but later commented to the War Cabinet on the slow rate of pillbox construction, which angered Gort when the news reached him via his chief engineer.

Chamberlain saw the Western Front as secure and thought no action there likely in the near future. During December he visited, assuring Gort in a letter towards the end of the month that Hore-Belisha's criticisms were now over. Indeed they were – Gort was surprised when Hore-Belisha left office in January. Hore-Belisha bitterly attributed that to being Jewish and therefore not acceptable to the Establishment.

Ironside failed to inform Gort of government decisions, and the Chiefs of Staff interfered in the BEF's leave arrangements without consulting Gort. Nor did Ironside inform the BEF's GHQ when their ammunition supply ceased in February. Brooke and Dill thought Gort accepted all this too easily – he did not complain or question an order. There was also still the question of his place in the chain of command, and which way the French would jump when things finally began to happen.

If Allied leadership was beset by quarrels, jealousies and uncertainty, at least more troops were on the way. The BEF's build-up continued during December 1939, 5th Infantry Division being the next to arrive, followed during early 1940 by the first two TA divisions – 48th (South Midland) and 50th (Northumbrian). In April, III Corps formed under Lieutenant General Sir Ronald Adam. This consisted of three TA divisions – the 12th, 23rd and 46th. Raised when the TA was ordered to be doubled, these new units were assigned to labouring duties. Their communications were hampered by the French, who, obsessed with security, insisted on radio silence.

The Army continued to expand, but there was still a chronic shortage of new equipment. Two units with the 1st Armoured Division give sad examples of this. The 9th Lancers, who trained during the winter at Wimborne in Dorset, were due to receive new cruiser tanks and finish their training in Normandy. They would be ordered to Southampton on 17 May, after fighting finally started, with only a few vehicles and with kit still arriving as they did so. C Squadron's CO would be seen driving down the Southampton road in his own car, handing out machine guns, telescopes and belt boxes to his crews as he went. Only half the tanks had been supplied to A Squadron, and its second-in-command had one armed with a 3-inch howitzer, for which there was no ammunition. Its Vickers machine gun lacked a telescopic sight. One second lieutenant's tank turret would be made of plywood, with no weapons other than the crew's personal ones.

The Queen's Bays trained in early 1940 with new Mark VIC light tanks – too lightly armed to engage heavier German armour and cursed with an equine rocking motion when travelling over rough ground. Receiving their sailing orders on 7 May, they did not reach Cherbourg until the 20th and then it was with three different types of cruiser tank, the Besa machine guns for which would only arrive at the last minute, still in their packing cases. The tanks' brake linings would wear out, making the vehicles difficult to steer, and there would be no time to net their wireless sets. Oh, and smoke ammunition would not be available.

Too little and too late. Is it any wonder the Germans had such an easy ride across northern France, once they had broken through the French line? All this calls to mind the saying that the British soldier can stand up to anything except the British government.

*   *   *

While the two sides had eyed each other on the Western Front, a very different war had been brewing in the Baltic. Stalin, as much an empire-builder as any of the Tsars, had taken over the Baltic states of Estonia, Latvia and Lithuania during the autumn months of 1939, gaining bases and a further buffer of territory against any future German expansion.

In October, claiming the war had changed the international situation, the Russians had invited Finland to begin discussing territorial arrangements. The Finns, having fought for their freedom not long before, rightly suspected that any 'renegotiation' would mean giving up ground. Helsinki ordered mobilisation on 9 October.

Demands and counterproposals went back and forth, with the Russian aim of a base on Finnish territory being rejected. Early in November Stalin ordered plans for an immediate war and on the 26th, in a situation reminiscent of the start of the Polish campaign, the Russians alleged that the Finns had fired on them. The Finns replied that any firing had come from the Russian side of the border. Diplomatic relations were broken off and the Russians invaded on the 30th.

Field Marshal Mannerheim, leading the Finnish Army and himself a former Tsarist officer, knew his 150,000-man force was too small to beat the Red Army on its own, but from the start the Finns were surprisingly successful, fighting amid snowy forests and frozen lakes against an army whose command structure had been weakened by Stalin's purges. The League of Nations called for a ceasefire, which Stalin rejected, and then expelled the Soviet Union as an aggressor – not that that made much difference. Against the odds, the Finns fought on, wiping out an entire Red Army division.

From Britain's point of view, should Stalin invade Scandinavia, his troops might not stop until they had established bases in northern Norway, which would not have been acceptable. There was also the question of Swedish iron ore supplies to Germany, through the ports of Lulea, on the Baltic, and Narvik, on the Norwegian coast. Lulea was ice-bound for four months of the year, but Narvik remained open and Norwegian waters provided a safe passage for German shipping.

Intervention in Finland would, therefore, go towards solving these problems, but the plans for this can best be described as too ambitious. Ironside, like Churchill, had fretted at the lack of activity and saw this as 'the one great strike which is open to us, to turn the tables upon the Russians and Germans'. However, within days he had reconsidered, warning the Cabinet not to act until their forces were ready. 'It is like putting a stick inside a hornet's nest without having provided yourself with a proper veil.'

Newall, Chief of the Air Staff, also saw the scheme as 'hare-brained'. Why should Norway and Sweden consent to their countries becoming battlegrounds? Gort was alarmed and angry, seeing this as neglect of the Western Front. The two British divisions earmarked for this operation never arrived, as permission to transport them through either Norway or Sweden was refused by those countries, neither of whom wished to become involved, or to see their profitable trade with Germany brought to a standstill.

By the middle of February the Finns were at last on the defensive, and a month later the war ended. The Russians gained most of their territorial demands at the cost of 68,000 dead. Finnish losses had been less than half that. The Red Army, and Hitler, took note. Britain and France were now off this hook, which was as well – they could not possibly have fought both Hitler and Stalin at once.

A sense of guilt at leaving the Finns to their fate led to the removal of Edouard Daladier as French Prime Minister. His replacement was the more aggressive Paul Reynaud – a step in the right direction but, again, too little and too late. Once again, thousands of lives had been lost and thousands more were to suffer, in spite of what the politicians said.

The British Chiefs of Staff now felt that the Germans would prefer Norwegian neutrality to having to invade. Should they try a landing on Norway's western coast, it would not succeed because of the Royal Navy's ships outnumbering them. It was also considered that Germany would not have enough resources to fight a war here and in western Europe as well.

Hitler, however, saw things very differently. On 14 December he had ordered the German High Command to 'investigate how one can take possession of Norway'. The previous summer he had met Vidkun Quisling, a former war minister and leader of the *Nasjonal Samling*, the Norwegian Nazi Party, who had encouraged the Germans to occupy his country. Quisling had also discussed this matter with Grossadmiral Raeder, and his name would later become a byword for treachery.

The *Altmark* incident further convinced Hitler that occupying Norway would be the only way to guarantee his iron ore supplies. Clearly the British could ignore neutrality when it suited them. The Führer's plans moved ahead, and with them the makings of an Allied disaster.

9

THROUGH DIFFICULTIES

The glorious thing about the flying service is that one feels that one is a perfectly free man and one's own master as soon as one is up in the air.

Manfred von Richthofen

In the rush to rearm that had taken place in the 1930s, the spectre of apocalyptic air raids had meant that priority had been given to fighter defence. This had not been entirely to the taste of the RAF's senior officers. The RAF's existence as a separate force depended, they felt, on providing, by strategic bombing, the means to reach into an enemy's backyard, where the Army and Navy could not go. Fighters had been seen as secondary.

To Chamberlain's government, however, they had been attractive. Providing an updated defence for your own country just might deter an enemy from attacking you. Anyway, the new Spitfires and Hurricanes were cheaper than bombers, using only one man per aircraft. Thankfully, in Sydney Camm of Hawkers and Reginald Mitchell of Supermarine, Britain had fighter designers who were second to none, although Mitchell, dying of cancer in 1937, had not lived long enough to see his most famous design go into service. Hurricanes joined the RAF at Northolt in West London in December 1937 – the Spitfire would join 19 Squadron at Duxford, near Cambridge, the following year.

Just how revolutionary these aircraft would be, compared with the fabric-covered biplanes that had preceded them, is shown by an incident that occurred at Duxford when the first Spitfire flew in. The pilot taxied to a stop, shutting off the engine. He then heard a pattering sound on the fuselage behind him and wondered why – there was no rain falling. It turned out to be a group of erks who, like curious natives confronted by something new, had walked up to the fighter and tentatively touched it. Then someone shouted, 'Good Lord, it's made of tin!' Indeed it was, unlike the Hurricane, whose construction was a halfway house between the old and the new. Nowadays no one would remark on it, but in 1938 it raised everybody's eyebrows.

These aircraft were fast and manoeuvrable, if not quite as agile as the biplanes that had preceded them, and their wings carried the unprecedented armament of eight Browning machine guns. It had been calculated by an RAF officer, Squadron Leader Ralph Sorley, that such heavy firepower would be needed for the few seconds they could expect to be on target.

A Spitfire Mark IA after landing. (IWM CH1448)

Backing up the new fighters was a defensive system that had been pushed forward since 1936 by Fighter Command's AOC, Air Chief Marshal Sir Hugh Dowding. Voice radio was available for communication and older pilots were being retrained as fighter controllers, whose domain would be the operations room – an earth-walled or semi-sunk building, quickly nicknamed 'the Hole', in which wooden counters, looking like something from a children's game, would be pushed across a giant map by airmen. Landlines, secure from any listening enemy, would provide further communication from Fighter Command to its groups covering the country. Part of the information was provided by the Observer Corps, consisting of civilians in small sandbagged outposts, checking on the height, course and identity of aircraft once they had crossed the coast.

The oddest parts of this system, leading to wild 'death ray' rumours, were the groups of 360-foot-high latticework towers springing up at intervals around the south and east coasts. They too were serviced by airmen who were learning a strange new language. It was all very hush-hush and these men were billeted separately from the others, just in case they talked in their sleep. A popular rumour that circulated when the first towers went up at Bawdsey in East Anglia was that if you drove your car too close to them the motor would stop!

This new system was called Radio Direction Finding – the implication being that it was some sort of navigational device – the acronym 'radar' had yet to be coined. The sites were known as the Chain Home network. No other country had anything like it, and the fighter pilots it was to guide knew little of it as yet.

In 1939 RDF was capable of detecting aircraft up to 15,000 feet and at over 100 miles away, regardless of weather. At this stage these sites were manned exclusively by men – Waafs would not come on the scene until the following year – and as it could not detect low flyers a new version, known as Chain Home Low, was being added.

RDF was also being ordered for anti-aircraft gun sites, to be known by the Army as 'Secret Wireless', but it would not be widely available for another year. Consequently sound locators had been deployed in two lines at 2-mile intervals on London's east flank, at right angles to the Thames. The Bawdsey research station, where all this had begun, had prepared for a move at the start of September, being subsequently dispersed to a variety of sites from Hampshire to Dundee. They would move again later, to Worth Matravers in Dorset and finally to Malvern in Worcestershire.

However, no system could stop the odd intruder getting through and remaining undetected. As noted in Chapter 1, on the morning war was declared the sirens wailed in London, for what was later described as a false alarm. A photograph reproduced here, taken over Buckingham Palace and the capital's centre, shows that there actually was a German reconnaissance aircraft over London that day. That was nothing new. Pre-war German reconnaissance flights had clandestinely photographed the south coast and London in the 1930s, often with the connivance of Deutsche Lufthansa, the German state airline, which had operated out of Croydon Airport until August 1939. Such photos, with significant targets carefully marked, would serve as 'before and after' markers for air raids in the years to come.

There was another hazard that this system could not guard against, and it surfaced on the morning of 6 September. At North Weald in Essex the Hurricane pilots of 56 and 151 Squadrons, collectively known as the North Weald Wing, were on standby from dawn.

The atmosphere in their dispersal hut would have tense, with a fear of the unknown. What was going to fall from the sky: bombs, gas or germ warfare? The uncertainty had been added to by German propaganda on the radio. If the bombers did come, an attack on London up the Thames estuary was their most likely route.

The drama began at 6.15 that morning when Army searchlight crews reported aircraft at high altitude near West Mersea in Essex. North Weald then scrambled both its squadrons in response. Lacking the practice that experience would later give them, the Hurricanes were delayed in getting airborne; and although 11 Group HQ had only ordered off one flight from 56, the entire squadron left the ground.

As 56 formed up to patrol the area between Harwich and Colchester at 11,000 feet, two other pilots took off in reserve aircraft and attempted to

B

Maßstab etwa 1: 15600

(1cm : 156 m)

London

1608

GB
Geheim

Bild:
467 R 51

vom
3. 3. 39.

Karte GB/E
1:100 000
Blatt 34

Länge
(westl.Greenw.):
0° 07' 30"
Nördl.Breite:
51° 30' 50"

Mißweisung:
- 10° 50'
(Mitte 1938)

Zielhöhe
über N N 30 m

1608

The centre of London, photographed by a German aircraft on the day Britain declared war – 3 September 1939. (N. J. Clarke)

catch up with them, the rest of the squadron being unaware that they were there. Group Captain D. F. Lucking, the sector controller, did not send back the other pilots, for the table in front of him was now filling up with plots of what appeared to be other incoming raids. 151 were now scrambled from North Weald, followed by 74 Squadron's Spitfires from Hornchurch, also in Essex. Flights from 54 and 65 Squadrons followed them into the air.

Leading 151 into the rising sun was Squadron Leader E. M. 'Teddy' Donaldson, who saw a large formation of aircraft ahead but was unable to identify them. His voice crackled over the radio. 'Bandits ahead, twelve o'clock. I believe they are friendly. Do not shoot unless positive identification.'

However, 74 Squadron had no doubts. The aircraft ahead were in a wide and loose Vic formation – the type the Germans were expected to adopt – and it was too large for a friendly flight. Also, behind and below were two more aircraft, which were taken to be the fighter escort. 74 Squadron's Red section dived to engage the 'enemy'. Donaldson, horrified, shouted over the radio, 'Do not retaliate. They are friendly!'

It was too late. The Hurricanes that were fired on split up, one gliding down in a left turn until it hit the ground. Donaldson angrily led the wing back to North Weald, where he was immediately told to contact Air Vice

Marshal Keith Park, AOC of 11 Group. Park informed Donaldson that he had arrested Group Captain Lucking, leaving Donaldson in command until a replacement could be appointed.

Pilot Officer Montagu Hulton-Harrop had been shot from behind and killed, crashing at Manor Farm, near Hintlesham. The first, but not the last, victim of 'friendly fire' in this war, he was twenty-six.

Pilot Officer Frank Rose, the other victim, was unwounded, but his Hurricane, hit in its cooling system, force-landed in a sugar beet field along the Ipswich–Manningtree road. A lorry driver, having seen him arrive, dashed over with his fire extinguisher. A dazed Rose told him that he thought he had been hit by another Hurricane, but was unsure. Staff from RAF Martlesham Heath checked over Rose's aircraft. An officer, knowing that German bullets had steel cores, as opposed to British lead ones, checked a wing for fragments. He found several lead ones, confirming Rose's suspicions.

Nor was that the end of the matter. Anti-aircraft gunners at Sheerness, Thameshaven and Chelmsford opened up, damaging a 65 Squadron Spitfire despite the correct recognition signal being flashed in Morse. This time the

Pilot Officer Montagu Hulton-Harrop of 56 Squadron – Fighter Command's first wartime casualty. (After The Battle)

pilot landed safely. It later turned out that the gunners, being young and inexperienced, were unable to read the signal.

Flying Officer Byrne and Pilot Officer Freeborn, who had fired on the two Hurricanes, were also arrested after returning to Hornchurch. They and Group Captain Lucking were later court-martialled, but acquitted. The whole affair became known as the Battle of Barking Creek, and although those airmen involved were forbidden to discuss the matter it did not take long for the Essex villagers to work out what had happened.

The Air Ministry and the Observer Corps took note. A check of the RDF site at Canewdon in Essex is said to have resulted in the discovery of a technical fault, in which aircraft flying inland from the station were transposed, making them appear to be coming in from the sea and therefore potentially hostile. Procedures in the telling of incoming plots were tightened up and the fitting of IFF to fighters was given increased priority. Both these measures came in time to benefit Fighter Command – and therefore the whole country – a year later.

For the moment, all the action seemed to be at home. During the first week of September, acting on a pre-war plan, the RAF moved its Advanced Air Striking Force, consisting of ten light bomber and two fighter squadrons, across to French airfields. 'Fields' were exactly what they were, with little more than grass and mud. The Air Component of the BEF – five squadrons of Lysanders and four of Hurricanes – followed.

The experience of 12 Squadron was typical. Previously known as 'Shiny Twelve', they now became 'The Dirty Dozen' – perhaps a comment on their new working conditions! Based at Amifontaine, near Rheims, the officers were fortunate to have the use of a chateau, while the NCOs were billeted in the nearby village. Their aircraft were dispersed under trees, a forest camouflaged a circle of airmen's tents, and one Nissen hut was available as an operations room.

It was hardly the welcome they had been expecting, especially as autumn turned to winter, with snow sweeping across the flat fields. Their feelings towards their hosts can be best summed up by a comment later made by the writer George Orwell:

> During the war of 1914–18 the English working class were in contact with foreigners to an extent that is rarely possible. The sole result was that they brought back a hatred of all Europeans, except the Germans, whose courage they admired. In four years on French soil they did not even acquire a liking for French wine.

This time their stay would be shorter, but their attitudes would be much the same.

Dowding had foreseen this deficiency and, although he had opposed supporting the BEF with any of his fighter squadrons at a time when their strength was being built up, he had ensured that it was only the

72 Squadron's pilots scrambling, for the benefit of the press, at Lille in November 1939. They would soon learn to disperse their Hurricanes around the airfield – parking aircraft in a neat line would present a tempting target for a strafing Bf 109. (IWM Neg. No. C465)

85 and 87 Squadrons' Hurricanes line up with two Gladiators and a Blenheim for a royal inspection at Seclin airfield near Lille. Despite Air Ministry regulations, 85's white hexagon and 87's arrow remain proudly displayed. (IWM Neg. No. F2344C)

Flight Lieutenant Ian Gleed, who served with 87 Squadron in France, pictured with his personal Figaro the Cat insignia. (IWM Neg. No. CH1639)

Hurricanes, with their strong broad-track undercarriages, that would make the crossing. Well designed though the Spitfire was, its more fragile undercarriage was less able to stand up to the rough treatment it was likely to receive over there.

The Hurricanes went across with outdated two-bladed wooden props, which limited their performance at altitude until supplies of more modern three-bladed variable pitch propellers became available. In the past, pilots had tended not to look behind – in the open-cockpit biplanes you would have lost your goggles if you did – but it was clear that the old tactic of getting on your opponent's tail was as valid as it had ever been. No one in authority had thought to provide mirrors, but wise men acquired their own from French garages. By mid-1940 they would become a standard fitting, as would armour behind the cockpit and bulletproof glass in front. For now, fighter pilots would have to make do without these aids to survival.

At this time the RAF's light bomber force, such as it was, consisted of Bristol Blenheims and Fairey Battles. On its introduction to service in 1937, the twin-engined Blenheim had looked like a winner, but the RAF was soon to find that by now the Bf 109 had caught up with it. It would not take German fighter pilots very long to find out that the single fin and rudder greatly restricted the dorsal gunner's field of fire to the rear, or that one machine gun in the turret was little defence against cannon. Although obsolete by 1941, it would have to soldier on overseas until the infinitely superior Mosquito arrived.

The Fairey Battle was an aircraft that ought never to have gone to war. Despite its sleek appearance, like an overgrown Hurricane, it proved a lumbering, wallowing pile of junk, carrying only a single Vickers K gun for rearward defence, and with no worthwhile bomb load. Its unfitness for combat was shown by the interception of three 88 Squadron Battles, which took off on reconnaissance from Mourmelon on 20 September. Bf 109s met them near the city of Aachen. Two were shot down, four men dying and two being injured. The sole surviving Battle's gunner claimed a Bf 109 shot down, which if true was the RAF's first air-to-air kill in this war. All this was an ominous pointer to the future.

In May 1940 most Battles would be destroyed on the ground or in the air, taking too many crews with them, leading to the few aircraft that remained being hurriedly withdrawn. Reallocated to engine test-bed use, or to pilot and gunnery training in peaceful Canadian skies, they would give far more valuable service there than they ever had in the line.

A Bristol Blenheim Mark IV on a test flight. The underwing serial numbers were deleted after war broke out. (Bristol Aeroplane Company)

A Fairey Battle of 142 Squadron, under a camouflage net on a French field – typical of the conditions the AASF had to face. (IWM)

A section of 218 Squadron's Battles over France. (IWM Neg. No. C447)

A gesture towards Army co-operation was shown by the inclusion of Westland Lysanders. This curious creation, with its high wings and spatted undercarriage, could not easily be mistaken for any other Allied aircraft. Brought in for reconnaissance, supply-dropping and liaison, it would eventually find its niche as a night-time agent-dropper, although that was all in the future.

Despite the opinion that the Ardennes forest would be impassable for armour, the possibility of an invasion through it and Luxembourg was quickly foreseen, as was German aggression against Belgium and Holland. Two plans were formed – the Scheldt and Dyle contingencies. For the first of these, the French 1st Groupe d'Armées, while securing French territory from Rochonvilliers to Maulde, was to establish itself on the Scheldt between Audenarde and Ghent. It was to occupy the area north and west of Antwerp, including the Scheldt's south bank. If necessary Flushing, South Beveland and Walcheren were to be included. The BEF would occupy the area from Maulde to Audenarde.

The Dyle contingency meant the French occupying the mouths of the Scheldt and advancing to the line Wavre–Gembloux–Namur. They were to link up with the BEF, holding the Dyle. The Belgians would hold the Antwerp area.

On 24 October Special Instruction No. 7 laid down the role of bomber forces in Belgium and Holland. Roads, bridges and airfields in these countries were marked as priority targets, as were the Rhine bridges at Wesel and Emmerich.

Already disquiet was being felt concerning the role of the RAF should such events occur. Air Commodore Norman Bottomley, SASO at Bomber Command headquarters, voiced it during October:

> The task for delaying advances of an enemy army is not one for which the bomber force has been trained. The general proposal to use bombers as one of the main instruments to check the advance of an unbroken enemy is a proposition of doubtful wisdom and the losses of our small bomber force are likely to be heavy in such an eventuality. Although bombers have proved extremely valuable in support of an advancing army, especially against weak anti-aircraft resistance, it is a very different matter to attempt to use a bomber force against an advancing army well supported by all forms of anti-aircraft defence and a large force of fighter aircraft. For this reason it should be made clear that the employment of our bombers against advancing troops will only be undertaken in extremis, and that otherwise our intention is the same as the French, i.e. to use our bombers 'with prudence'.
>
> The Battles and the Blenheims are the only aircraft which could be profitably or economically used against columns of troops, columns of AFVs and motorised columns at the head of an advancing army. The Hampdens and Wellingtons would be more profitably employed against permanent objectives further in the rear and against railroad junctions and railroad concentrations, say, in the area between the Rhine and the Meuse.

Whatever the future might bring, responsibilities had to be decided now. The Air Component's reconnaissance aircraft were to share tasks with the French Air Force. Its Lysanders were to work exclusively for the BEF, with its Hurricanes escorting operations within the BEF's zone. There would be direct liaison between the fighter squadrons and French intelligence centres at Lille, Amiens and Dunkirk, allowing information to be passed between the two while the French benefited from RDF. A central operations room was completed on 14 October, but it was noted, 'This work would have been completed several days earlier had not the same working party also been employed on the construction of the offices of the General Commanding and of his Chief of Staff.'

Relations between the RAF and the Army remained controversial. The BEF wanted its own air arm, arguing, not unreasonably, that as it was they who were being supported they ought to have some say in the matter. The RAF, anxious as always to preserve its independence, was happy to help them but would not accept BEF control of the AASF as well.

While the fighter boys and those around them learned the lesson of Barking Creek, what of the bomber crews? Dropping leaflets over German cities was not what they had trained for, yet they were forbidden from using bombs, in case of massive German retaliation. When Conservative MP Leo Amery suggested doing something useful, such as setting the Black Forest on fire, the Air Minister, Sir Kingsley Wood, was most upset. 'Are you aware it is private property? Why, you will be asking me to bomb Essen next.' Since that Ruhr city was the home of the Krupp steel works, it would indeed have been a worthwhile target, but for now the gloves remained on.

The War Cabinet, noting the lack of results from the early raids on Wilhelmshaven and Brunsbüttel, directed that in future bombers would confine their attacks to warships at sea, and not attempt to penetrate heavily defended naval bases. Reconnaissance missions by single Coastal Command aircraft over the Heligoland Bight had achieved nothing, partly due to faulty radios and the fact that, even if they had promptly got through, by the time any bombers had arrived their targets would have returned to harbour. So, from 26 September a new policy of reconnaissance in force was tried.

Three days later eleven Hampden bombers took off from RAF Hemswell in Lincolnshire. One section of five, led by the CO, were all shot down by Bf 109s between the islands of Heligoland and Wangerooge. Of the twenty men aboard, only four survived, to be taken prisoner. The other six found two German destroyers, bombing them without result.

Prien's sinking of *Royal Oak* brought an increase in German air reconnaissance off Scotland's east coast. After the battlecruiser *Hood* was seen making for Rosyth, Göring's chief-of-staff, Hans Jeschonnek, rang Hauptmann Helmut Pohle of KG30 at their Westerland base to order an attack. However, he included a warning. 'Should the *Hood* already be in dock when KG30 reaches the Firth of Forth, no attack is to be made. I make you personally responsible for acquainting every single crew with this order. The Führer won't have a single civilian killed.'

It makes strange reading after the savagery of the Polish campaign, and is an example of Hitler's curious attitude to Britain. On the one hand he loathed those, such as Churchill, who had seen through and stood up to him. On the other he was inclined to see the British as fellow Aryans, who he had no wish to fight. It was an attitude that many of his countrymen shared at this time. Chamberlain, and most of his government, were no better than old women, with no stomach for war. There was every chance that they would see sense and sue for peace before long.

The Junkers Ju 88A-1 had been hailed as the Luftwaffe's 'Wonder Bomber'. Of more recent design than the Heinkel 111 or the Dornier 17, it was fast and ruggedly built, as befitted a company that had pioneered all-metal construction a generation ago. At the rear of its crew's canopy was a single 7.92-mm machine gun as defence and, to facilitate a rapid escape, the rear part of the canopy was detachable by pulling a lever in the cockpit.

At two o'clock on the afternoon of 16 October, Hauptmann Pohle led nine Ju 88s at 12,000 feet over Edinburgh towards the Firth of Forth and its famous railway bridge – another tempting target but, like bridges everywhere, almost impossible to hit. *Hood,* frustratingly, was in Rosyth's sea-lock, on her way into the inner harbour. Never mind, there were the cruisers *Edinburgh* and *Southampton* moored offshore, in company with the destroyer *Mohawk*. Pohle dived through a storm of flak to release his bomb, gasping as the rear part of his canopy suddenly came away, exposing the crew to a draught and taking the single rear gun with it. The bomb passed through three of *Southampton*'s decks, emerging through the cruiser's side to sink a launch moored alongside her.

Pohle had been assured by German intelligence that there were no Spitfires based in the area. They did not know that two Auxiliary units, 602 and 603 Squadrons, having recently re-equipped with them, were eager to prove themselves. Their base, Turnhouse, near Edinburgh, was only a short distance away.

All of a sudden the sky seemed full of darting shark-like shapes with broad tapered wings. The bomber juddered as Flight Lieutenant George Pinkerton set Pohle's port engine on fire, also hitting his rear gunner and wireless operator. The next pass injured his observer. Trying to reach home, Pohle spotted a trawler and, thinking it might be a neutral Norwegian one, ditched near to it. Instead, he was rescued by a destroyer, collapsing on its deck with concussion and facial injuries.

Pohle came to a few days later in the Royal Navy hospital at Port Edward, near Edinburgh. Evidently still suffering from concussion, he at first thought he was in Norway, asking a nurse if he could make a phone call to Italy. Eventually he was made to understand where he was, and that

South Queensferry and the Forth railway bridge, photographed by a German reconnaissance aircraft on 2 October 1939. (Royal Commission on the Ancient and Historical Monuments of Scotland)

The Luftwaffe's eye-view of British warships under attack on 16 October. (After The Battle)

his fellow crew members had not survived. After preliminary interrogation by an RAF officer, his next stop was another hospital at Edinburgh Castle, then south to the Tower, and finally to Grizedale Hall.

Hit by 603's Red section, Oberleutnant H. Storp's Ju 88 also ditched 4 miles off Port Seton. He and two of his crew, all injured, were picked up by the trawler *Day Spring*, for which Storp gave John Dickson, the skipper, a signet ring. On landing they were taken to Port Seton police station, no doubt being subjected to curious stares by the population. Leutnant H. von Rosen's aircraft was also hit by 603, but safely reached home.

Two Ju 88s had been lost, one to each squadron, with only minimal damage to one of their three offshore targets. Dowding sent his congratulations. 'Well done. First blood to the Auxiliaries.' This made the regulars keener than ever.

It was a time when a measure of chivalry could still be observed. Pinkerton visited Pohle in hospital and his ground crew acted as pallbearers at the funeral of two of the crew, who were interred with full military honours in Edinburgh's Portobello Cemetery. The good citizens of Edinburgh and Dunfermline, however, were less inclined to be charitable. There had been no warning before the raid, leading those who had watched it at first to see it as a practice. Shrapnel from the guns had fallen in the streets, causing two casualties.

At this time, scrambles of sections of fighters frequently occurred off the east coast, with three aircraft chasing a solitary aircraft either on reconnaissance or mine-laying. On 17 October, Oberfeldwebel Eugen Lange was the pilot of a Heinkel 111 of 2(F)/122 on reconnaissance to the Firth of Forth. Reaching it at 19,000 feet, but finding the area cloud-covered, with three Spitfires just above it, they decided to turn away and return later. Flying north for the second time, 8 miles east of Whitby they were spotted by Green section of 41 Squadron, whose Spitfires chased them out to sea for another 12 miles.

Leutnant Joachim Kretschmer, the observer, and Unteroffizier Hugo Sauer, the flight engineer, were both killed. A stream of tracer from the Heinkel's dorsal position stopped when Unteroffizer Bernard Hochstuhl, the observer, took a bullet in the leg. Bullets grazed his flying helmet and Lange's earphones. With both engines hit they had no choice but to ditch. Lange and Hochstuhl scrambled into their dinghy, still alive but without food and drink. The impact had stopped Lange's watch at five o'clock.

The Spitfires circled overhead, radioing their position, but eventually departed the scene for their base at Catterick, knowing there was nothing else they could do. Although the two survivors fired Very lights during the two nights that followed, and the lifeboats at Whitby and Runswick Bay had seen them, the dinghy could not be located. Forty-three hours later, wet, cold and miserable, the survivors drifted ashore into a cove just north of the coastal village of Sandsend.

By now Lange was suffering from exposure, so Hochstuhl, despite his wound, climbed a goat track to the Whitby–Middlesbrough coastal railway line. He still thought they were near the Firth of Forth and had no idea of their present position. LNER Special Constable George Thomas, who had been patrolling the line, was suddenly confronted by a bedraggled figure in flying kit, who he took to Sandsend station. The constable did his best to assure Hochstuhl that his friend would be looked after, and indeed both survived, Lange after being lugged up the cliff by Thomas, with another policeman from the nearby village of Lythe and a Sandsend painter, the three of them using the dinghy as a stretcher.

The stationmaster's wife offered them food and drink, but such was the state they were in that neither was able to swallow very much. Hochstuhl gave Thomas his cigarettes as a token of gratitude. Thomas was later quoted as saying, 'They were quite decent fellows. One of them said, "I don't know what we're fighting for." I shall not smoke these cigarettes, but I may have one when there is somebody else in charge in Germany and peace is declared.' However, he never did smoke them.

Both men were taken to Whitby police station, where Lange was treated to a hot bath, and then to the local hospital, where they were placed in separate rooms, each guarded by an Army corporal. Sister Winifred Wilson found Hochstuhl appreciative – he gave her his Luftwaffe wings badge as a souvenir, but Lange was stiff and suspicious, initially refusing his medication and apparently under the impression that the staff were out to poison him. After two days both travelled by train to London and a POW camp, first in Britain, then Canada. They were the first Germans to be taken prisoner in England in this war.

During October, KG26's Heinkel 111s also carried out reconnaissance over what Luftwaffe crews had now christened 'the watery triangle' – the North Sea. These thousand-mile flights called for a high degree of navigation skill and vigilance. The Heinkels carried cameras in place of their port bomb racks, thus enabling them to attack shipping if the opportunity arose.

On 28 October, Leutnant Rolf Niehoff and his crew set off from Westerland. This time their target was the Firth of Clyde, of increased interest following the Home Fleet's withdrawal to western Scotland after Prien's attack. They also crossed the Firth of Forth, but were unable to photograph it due to cloud. Apart from aircraft already on patrol, 602 Squadron's Yellow section was ordered off to pursue Niehoff's Heinkel as it passed over the base at Drem. They failed to make contact, but did spot another twin-engined aircraft near May Island, in the Forth. Unfortunately for all concerned this was an RAF Anson. Flight Lieutenant Hodge, leading the section, ordered them to break off, but not before the Anson's pilot had

The Humbie Heinkel 111. (IWM Neg. No. HU5518)

been wounded in the jaw. Excitement had made the pilots see what they wished to see.

Niehoff, on returning over the Forth at a lower altitude, found HMS *Edinburgh*, *Southampton* and *Mohawk* were still there. The cloud had thinned, but while this improved the prospects for photography it also made his bomber a clearer target for the naval anti-aircraft gunners, one of whose first shells exploded near the fuselage. The flak bursts also alerted a section each from 602 and 603, who were patrolling in the area.

On German bombers the observer was in charge if he outranked the pilot. Niehoff ordered Unteroffizier Kurt Lehmkuhl to make for the cloud below them. It was not thick enough, and 602, diving from their patrol height of 10,000 feet, reached the Heinkel first, attacking in line astern. 603, initially higher at 14,000 feet, followed them.

Lehmkuhl remained in control despite being hit twice in his back. Behind him the gunners, Gefreiter Bruno Rehmann and Unteroffizier Gottlieb Kowalke, were shot dead as they changed ammunition drums. Now at a low height and with both engines smoking, a crash-landing amid the Lammermuir Hills was inevitable. Despite his pain, Lehmkuhl slowed the Heinkel down to landing speed, the impact coming just before it would have stalled.

The bomber struck a hillside between High Latch and Kidlaw, east of Humbie village, ploughing through a dry stonewall. Tearing off its starboard tailplane, it bounced and thumped for several yards uphill, coming to rest with its back broken and nose smashed open.

Noise changed abruptly to quiet. Once he had collected himself, Niehoff helped Lehmkuhl out into the surrounding heather. Local farm workers, whose language he did not understand, were first on the scene, followed by police. Lehmkuhl was carried to the nearest road on a gate used as a stretcher. Niehoff was taken to a police station, then to the country estate headquarters of an Army unit. After all he had just been through, it was strange to be entertained to lunch! That afternoon he faced an interrogation by RAF officers at Edinburgh Castle's guardroom, then it was south by train to the Tower of London. Here it was discovered that he had broken his back during the impact. Four months of treatment in Woolwich Hospital followed, before he was sent to Grizedale Hall. Like so many other prisoners taken in the first year of war, Niehoff would later be shipped to Canada.

The two Spitfire squadrons were awarded a joint kill, and, although the RAF quickly roped off the crash area, this new spectacle attracted small boys of two to seventy-two, with not a few souvenir-hunters among them. The Heinkel looked like an enormous dead shark, its dark upper surfaces liberally spattered with 0.303-inch bullet holes, each with an accompanying ragged silver halo where the paint had been burned off. In the district no one spoke of anything else, and for children it was exciting. Yes, they were real, they did come over here, and they did wear black crosses.

The Heinkel was soon dismembered by the RAF's 63 Maintenance Unit, its airframe going to the Royal Aircraft Establishment at Farnborough, where everything, down to individual instruments, was thoroughly checked over, resulting in a long report that was not completed until 1941. A collection of items from the aircraft can be seen today in the Scottish United Services Museum at Edinburgh Castle.

The fighter boys, at home and abroad, seemed to be determined to live up to their glamorous reputation. It was personified by Pilot Officer 'Cobber' Kain, of 73 Squadron. A New Zealander in his early twenties, Kain looked the part and lived up to it. His first kill was a Dornier 17 on reconnaissance, which he had seen above and ahead while on patrol. Kain was to destroy fourteen aircraft while in France and would have been an asset to any Battle of Britain squadron had he not died wastefully when indulging in low-level aerobatics over his home airfield.

It was quickly found that friendly fire was not confined to those squadrons still at home. Already the Hurricanes serving in France were painted half black and half white underneath. Now, as a further distinction, they started carrying red, white and blue stripes in French style on their rudders. Never mind the enemy, defend me from my friends.

Not all those going to France would do so in shiny new monoplanes. 615 Squadron, an Auxiliary unit referred to as 'Churchill's Own' since he was its honorary air commodore, still had Gladiators in November 1939 when he paid them a visit. As expected, Churchill took a particular interest in the four guns carried by the aircraft flown by Flight Lieutenant James 'Sandy' Sanders. As her husband stood in front of the aircraft, Mrs Churchill climbed into its cockpit and started to toy with the firing mechanism. Sanders, realising the guns were not only loaded but also cocked, averted a tragedy that would have altered the course of British history!

U-boats and mines were taking a mounting toll of British shipping, leading Churchill to become more aggressive. Why, he demanded, did the RAF not venture to Wilhelmshaven? Consequently Bomber Command was ordered to mount 'a major operation with the object of destroying an enemy battlecruiser or pocket battleship'. Although there was no longer any restriction on attacking warships in the vicinity of their bases, care still had to be taken to ensure that no bombs fell on land. Warships could not be attacked if they were in dock or berthed alongside quays.

Bomber Command's response on 3 December was to send twenty-four Wellingtons from 38, 115 and 149 Squadrons to the island fortress of Heligoland, their object being to attack any enemy warship there. Each aircraft carried four 500-pound semi-armour-piercing bombs. 149 Squadron's CO, Wing Commander R. Kellett, led twelve aircraft from Mildenhall in Suffolk. He would reconnoitre the target first. Meeting up over Thetford in Norfolk, the squadrons flew out towards Denmark. On receipt of a coded message that cruisers were at Heligoland, the sections

A preserved Gloster Gladiator at a post-war air show. The last of the RAF's biplane fighters, it would face the Luftwaffe in Norway in 1940. (Author's collection)

of three aircraft swung round after passing within 3 miles of it, round the west side and to the north, at over 10,000 feet.

Pilot Officer H. A. Innes, second pilot in one of 149's Wellingtons, was amazed, not just to be going on a live bombing raid this time, but at the fact that despite there being a clear sky at this point, there was no flak either – though it began as they ran into some cloud over the ships seen between two islands. At this time the RAF had no bomb aimers – that job fell to the second pilot, who had become a maid-of-all-work. Prone in the nose and intent on his bombing run, Innes did not notice the flak, now intense, aimed at his leader. The stick setting for his load had been incorrectly set, so all four left the bomb-bay at once instead of one after the other.

Possibly summoned by a patrolling ship, a total of twenty-eight Messerschmitt 109s from five different units rose in defence, though only four of them, from I/JG26, caught up with the bombers, by now 5 miles away from the harbour. They met an enthusiastic response from the rear gunners, and as red tracer wobbled out towards the enemy one of them went down trailing black smoke but pulled out before hitting the sea and flew off. Leutnant Gunter Specht lost his left eye but survived. This damage was credited to LAC Copley of 38 Squadron, himself fortunate to survive when a bullet struck the quick-release box on his parachute harness.

All the Wellingtons returned safely, claiming one hit on a cruiser. One 115 Squadron Wellington had a bomb hang-up over the harbour. It then fell away to explode on land – the first RAF bomb to do so on German soil in this war.

After just over five hours in the air, the tired crews were now subjected to interrogation by their intelligence officers. Logs had to be handed in and forms made out. Innes went to Mildenhall's operations room to be questioned by its group captain, then he was made to repeat it all over a phone to a senior officer of the Air Staff. He was sure that he had hit the largest ship there. After that, it was an early night.

Innes soon realised the nature of this method of waging war. His only concern had been the target, not anyone aboard it. From that height, it might as well have been a mark on the ground, like one on a range that he had aimed practice bombs at. Any loss of life he might have caused did not trouble him. It was that impersonal.

The damage he claimed was not supported by German records. Apart from Specht's Bf 109, one trawler converted into a minesweeper had been sunk by a bomb that had passed through it without exploding. A flak position had been damaged by the hung-up bomb, but without casualties. A German report described the raid as 'cleverly delivered from the sun and executed with great certainty in avoiding the residential area of the island'.

From the Air Staff's point of view, it looked as if the theory of the self-defending bomber formation had held up. These aircraft had satisfactorily defended one another. Fire from their rear and ventral turrets had shot down one fighter while driving off three others, which had come no closer than 600 yards.

If this was the best the Luftwaffe could do, then even the lumbering Whitleys stood a chance of surviving by day. During the next ten days, shipping searches were tried, with all three types of RAF bomber taking part, but without success. On the 12th eight Whitleys flew evening patrols over suspected seaplane bases on the islands of Sylt, Nordeney and Borkum, their object being to harass the mine-carrying Heinkel 115s operating from there. These operations were flown on seventeen nights until the middle of January, bombs being dropped on water whenever flarepath lights were shown. Other targets were a U-boat and a flak ship, but no results were seen.

The next round came about when the submarine HMS *Salmon* torpedoed the cruisers *Nürnberg* and *Leipzig* on 13 December. As the German vessels limped back to Wilhelmshaven, Bomber Command was instructed to finish them off. A force of Hampdens found nothing after taking off at dawn on the 14th. Later in the morning they were followed by twelve 99 Squadron Wellingtons from Newmarket, whose racecourse had now become an airfield.

Each Wellington carried three 500-pound SAP bombs, which would not penetrate armoured decks unless dropped from at least 2,000 feet. They had been ordered not to bomb unless they could see their targets from that height.

Flying in sections of three, the crews sighted Terschelling just after one in the afternoon and turned northwards as though making for Heligoland.

No one yet knew that the Germans were now beginning to use Freya
ground radar, with a range of a hundred miles.

A low cloud base had now forced the crews down to 200 feet, just below
it, when they saw a submarine, which crash-dived. Then, as they now flew
north-east, two cruisers appeared out of the murk, steaming south about
a mile away. The leader, Wing Commander J. F. Griffiths, turned north to
check them for torpedo damage. One was the *Nürnberg*, doing 10 knots,
but he passed by too quickly for any damage assessment. It was when
Griffiths turned his squadron onto the same southerly heading that they
met heavy flak from the cruisers and three escorting destroyers.

He aborted the attack and turned for home. Too low – at this height
the bombs would bounce off. No sense in risking lives for that. Up ahead,
Wangerooge island loomed up in the mist and from it rose three black
specks. From JG77, these were Bf 109E-1s, the latest version. Worse still,
accompanying them was a *Schwarme* of Messerschmitt Bf 110s from
2/ZG26. A fast twin-engined fighter, the Bf 110 was armed with a
formidable battery of cannon and machine guns in its nose. It was about
to see action for the first time.

Forming up in line astern, the fighters attacked the last section of three
Wellingtons, with flak from ships around Wangerooge joining in. Sergeant
Brace's aircraft fell in flames towards the sea and Flying Officer Cooper
swung away towards the German coast, lowering his undercarriage – either

The Messerschmitt Bf 109E, a fighter that would rule European skies after proving itself
in Spain. (Author's collection)

a sign of surrender or damaged hydraulics. It made no difference, for they never reached the shore.

The rear and ventral turrets fired back, sending a Bf 109 into the sea. A Bf 110 dived on the leader, but sheered off after its rear gunner, Corporal Bickerstaff, sent tracer through the cockpit. In the second section Flight Lieutenant Brough's crew fought off another Bf 110.

To port and behind the leader, Pilot Officer Lewis turned back, colliding with Sergeant Downey in the section behind him. Flight Sergeant Healey's aircraft turned over in flames, showing the fabric burned away underneath to expose the geodetic structure. Those who survived bullets or cannon shells were claimed by the North Sea.

The action lasted for 26 minutes, but to the gunners it probably seemed much longer. Two guns each against a sky full of darting grey shapes, and their sole protection only one piece of armour on the rear turret's outside. Also, before the era of ammunition channels in the fuselage, they were depending on another crew member running back with spare ammunition boxes. Five hundred rounds per turret did not go far in a fight like this.

The attack ended as quickly as it had begun, but the dying was not over. Flight Lieutenant Hetherington, from the rear section, caught up with the others before they arrived home, but on reaching Newmarket crashed in a nearby field, killing himself and two other crew members.

It added up to six Wellingtons lost and thirty-three crew members dead. For what? One fighter lost. The Bf 109 pilots correctly claimed five Wellingtons down, with Hetherington's aircraft as a probable. Their one loss was admitted. The Bf 110s seemed not to have scored – but they would have ample chance to do so within days.

News of the losses quickly reached 149 Squadron at Mildenhall. Pilot Officer Innes noted that in most cases it was the Wellington's port wing that had caught alight after its unarmoured fuel tanks had been hit. Astonishingly, it seems that only the starboard ones had been protected.

As bad was the reluctance of senior officers to face facts, among them Air Commodore Norman Bottomley, who in a letter afterwards attributed the losses to flak and doubted if the fighters had scored at all:

[The] failure of the enemy must be ascribed to good formation flying. The maintenance of tight, unshaken formation in the face of the most powerful enemy action is the test of bomber force fighting efficiency and morale. In our service it is the equivalent of the old 'Thin Red Line' or the 'Shoulder to Shoulder' of Cromwell's Ironsides.

Now it was a thin blue line of airmen who were facing the worst the Luftwaffe could do. Even a 50 per cent loss did not bring about a change in attitudes. Bottomley, far away from the action in Bomber Command headquarters at High Wycombe and reluctant to be proved wrong, chose to ignore the bullet holes visible in the surviving Wellingtons.

Someone who was nearer the mark was the crews' AOC. Air Vice Marshal Jackie Baldwin of 3 Group likened the affair to the Charge of the Light Brigade. Nevertheless, on 17 December Baldwin called Bottomley to urge a further attack on the German fleet. Although noted for his sensitivity to casualties, Air Chief Marshal Sir Edgar Ludlow-Hewitt, AOC Bomber Command, agreed, provided the Wellingtons bombed from 10,000 feet, which ought to take them above most flak.

Twenty-four Wellingtons were to take part – nine from 149 Squadron, nine from 9 Squadron at RAF Honington in Suffolk and six from 37 Squadron at RAF Feltwell in Norfolk. All were tasked to attack warships in the Schillig Roads or Wilhelmshaven. However, the gloves were still on: 'Great care is to be taken that no bombs fall on shore, and no merchant ships are to be attacked. Formations shall not loiter in the target area, and all aircraft are to complete bombing as soon as possible after the sighting signal has been made.'

This showed some acknowledgement of reality. No sane crew would loiter – not now. News of 99 Squadron's losses had travelled fast across the bomber country of East Anglia.

Crews were to stand by early on the morning of 18 December. Weather reconnaissance was provided by a 78 Squadron Whitley, which at eight

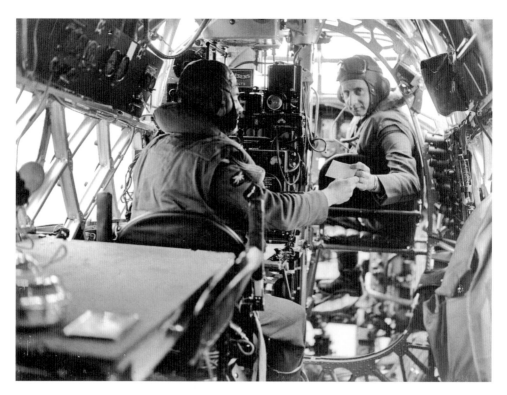

The interior of a 215 Squadron Wellington, with the wireless operator handing a message to the second pilot. (IWM Neg. No. CH79)

that morning reported patchy cloud near Heligoland – ideal conditions for a daylight raid.

Once again Richard Kellett would lead. Although an experienced airman, having won an AFC after leading three Wellesley monoplanes on a non-stop flight from Ismailia to Darwin in 1938 – setting a long-distance record – Kellett had only recently joined 149 Squadron, having never flown with either 9 or 37. Although 9 had practised the formation of three aircraft in a section, 37, which had yet to see action, had developed a looser arrangement of aircraft in pairs, each leader to the left and ahead of his number two. 3 Group had never practised any group formation flying. Squadron Leader Paul Harris of 149 was later to describe this as 'a fatal error'.

What resulted was a far cry from the drilled and disciplined formations that the US 8th Air Force would later practise in those same East Anglian skies before setting out for Europe. Kellett's task could be likened to getting three different orchestras to play the same piece together when all had rehearsed it separately at different speeds.

After taking off, 149 and 9 Squadrons rendezvoused over King's Lynn, as arranged. An hour later 37 Squadron caught up with them over the sea. The plan was to avoid flak ships off the Frisian Islands, as they were thought to have previously passed on a warning. The fact of German radar was unknown as yet.

As they climbed to 14,000 feet the cloud thinned out until, in spite of what the Whitley crew had said, the sky looked like blue silk. Not a scrap of cover left. It was cold too, with icy draughts blowing down each unheated fuselage – cold that numbed despite gloves and fleece-lined Irvin jackets.

The formation was now spread out in a big diamond. Kellett and Flight Lieutenant Duguid led the first two sections. To their right and rear came Squadron Leader Paul Harris with 149's third section, then a section from 9 behind him. To their left were 9's other six aircraft. Behind them 37 followed in three echelon formations of two aircraft each.

Two aircraft would drop out early. Duguid could not maintain the revs on his starboard engine, so, being unable to hold his position, he signalled by Aldis lamp to his numbers two and three. Flying Officer Riddlesworth correctly closed up on Kellett, but Flight Sergeant Kelly misunderstood, turning away from the formation to follow Duguid home.

After three hours the remaining aircraft turned south on seeing Sylt, now running down the coast of Schleswig-Holstein. Now radar picked them up, an hour away from their target.

The Germans nearly missed this opportunity. In November Oberstleutnant Carl Schumacher had become Geschwaderkommodore of JG1, established to defend this part of Germany's North Sea coast. His request for reinforcements after the raid a fortnight before had been met by the addition of I/ZG76's Bf 110 fighters, veterans of the Polish campaign. Now he had up to a hundred aircraft, controlled from Jever, a few miles west of Wilhelmshaven. 'Splendid weather for fighters,' observed Schumacher to his adjutant, Leutnant Miller-Trimbusch, who replied, 'The Tommies are not such fools – they won't come today.'

On this day the newly arrived 2nd Staffel of I/ZG76, under its Staffelkapitän, Wolfgang Falck, was exercising near Borkum, giving the local radar station a chance to demonstrate its Freya set to a visiting naval officer. Then a further large blip appeared, coming from Sylt. Leutnant Hermann Diehl promptly phoned Jever, but was told, 'You're plotting seagulls or there's interference on your set.' Twenty minutes later the Kriegsmarine Freya set on Heligoland also picked up Kellett's formation.

In 1939 the German warning organisation was beset by arguments between the Luftwaffe and Kriegsmarine over who should control which area, making inter-Service communication a problem. The Heligoland report was passed, though not with any urgency, through the Kriegsmarine headquarters exchange to the Luftwaffe at Jever. It took the better part of an hour to get things moving – an hour granted by the route Kellett had taken. Then observers on Heligoland reported them as forty-four aircraft – double the actual number and probably a repetition during transmission. Finally a scramble order went out from Jever.

First on the scene were six night-fighting Bf 109D-1s from 10(N)/JG26, whose report of their course, height and speed brought I/ZG76's Bf 110s and II/JG77's Bf 109s, of whom Unteroffizier Heilmayr was the first to go in. As the bombers turned north for Wilhelmshaven, 9 Squadron's six aircraft on their left side were left behind and struggling to catch up. Falck and Unteroffizier Fresia went for this group. The Staffelkapitän's victim blew up under the lash of his cannon shells, while the other fell away with its port engine on fire. Then Falck chased Squadron Leader Guthrie, whose rear gunner responded with a burst into his starboard engine, filling the cockpit with smoke. However, again Falck's shells had found their mark, sending Guthrie's Wellington down towards the grey sea below. Fresia attacked Flying Officer Allison, who also plunged into the sea with a blazing port wing.

Though out of the fight, Falck's troubles were not over. While heading back for Jever his port engine cut as well. Firing off the rest of his ammunition and jettisoning fuel to lighten the aircraft, he glided as far as Wangerooge, making a skilful 'deadstick' landing. 'That was the first and last time I became a glider pilot,' he later commented.

To the right and rear of Guthrie was Flying Officer Bill Macrae, a tough, hard-drinking Canadian, who cursed on hearing his rear gunner declare he could not get his guns to bear due to frozen fingers. Bullets gashed his fuselage and wings, leaking fuel from their tanks. Sergeant Petts, after vainly calling his leader to slow down, dived to sea level rather than fall further behind, suddenly closing his throttles so that the fighters overshot. With two wounded gunners he flew 200 miles to RAF Sutton Bridge in Lincolnshire, landing safely despite a burst tyre. Macrae reached the coastal airfield at North Coates Fitties.

Paul Harris, on the starboard side, had told 9's section leader, Flight Lieutenant Peter Grant, 'Stick close to me whatever happens.' Grant obeyed, keeping together a formation of six whose guns drove off attempts to get in close. However, cannon outranged the Brownings, allowing the fighters to score from further out. As fuel poured from a wing tank, Grant transferred what was left. To port of him Sergeant Hewitt was suffering in an identical manner, also with jammed turrets and a mortally wounded rear gunner.

The night-fighters could not stay out of this. Remembering that the Wellington's turrets could not cover a beam attack, Oberleutnant Johann Fuhrmann attacked three times in this manner, but his deflection shooting was poor and he missed each time. Finally he came in from behind, was hit and ditched just off the island of Spiekeroog, drowning when he tried to swim ashore in his heavy flying suit. Impatience had proved fatal.

Now a Bf 110 shot across Kellett's aircraft, destroying Flying Officer Speirs in a ball of flame. Determined to keep together, Kellett, Harris and Grant led their survivors out to sea.

It really was devil take the hindmost now, with 37 Squadron suffering more than anyone else. Squadron Leader Hue-Williams caught up with those in front just as Oberleutnant Gordon Gollob's Bf 110 dived. Hue-Williams went down with his starboard wing blazing. Flying Officer Lemon dived for the sea, pursued by II/JG77's Leutnant Roman Stiegler. To his rear gunner's amazement, Stiegler's wingtip hit the sea and in he went. Lemon flew home just above the waves. His Wellington was the only one of 37 Squadron to return to Feltwell.

Sergeant Ruse's aircraft, hit by Oberleutnant Helmut Lent's Bf 110, had two crew killed. Now he needed to get down, and fast. Skidding to a halt amid Borkum's sand dunes, the three survivors, one of them wounded, climbed out to be taken prisoner. Lent then hit Flying Officer Thompson's Wellington, reporting that it hit the sea with both engines burning. On impact it broke up and sank.

Flying Officers Wimberley and Lewis had headed west over the Schillig Roads. Finished off by Lent after other attacks, Wimberley ditched his aircraft, being the only one to struggle out through its cockpit roof hatch. Lewis and his crew all died in a crash on the mud flats off Spiekeroog.

It had all taken just twenty minutes. Now the sky was suddenly clear. And for those who had come through, it was a time to wipe away sweat, despite the cold, and to take deep breaths through dry mouths. Time for an intercom check – if it still worked – to restock ammunition at the rear and to look over the fuel state.

They were still alive, but would they reach home? Sergeant Hewitt and Flying Officer Briden were gradually dropping back due to damage, with the sea getting closer. Harris ordered his navigator to check an apparent injury to their front gunner, but it had only been a bullet clipping the heel from his flying boot. His concern now was whether he would have to fork out for a new pair. The rum flask Harris passed round put new life into all of them, though on reaching the rear turret it remained there until the aircraft landed.

Briden and Hewitt were not so fortunate, both ditching off Norfolk. Harris tried to drop his dinghy to Briden, but was unable to detach it from his aircraft, forcing him to land at Coltishall, a new RAF fighter base. The Cromer lifeboat failed to find this crew. Hewitt and three others were rescued by the trawler *Erillas* after scrambling from their sinking bomber, leaving behind the body of LAC Lilley.

That made twelve Wellingtons lost. Apart from the two Bf 109s at sea, two others had been damaged, one of them being written off after a crash landing.

Why had the British come on so clear a day, and for what? The mystery was added to when the wreck of Ruse's aircraft turned out to have an empty bomb bay. A training exercise? Some sort of semi-suicidal daylight reconnaissance? That was not far from the truth, but the Germans were further confused by the lies told by Ruse and Wimberley during interrogation. No one seemed to have seen Ruse dump his load before crashing, or consider that he might have done so.

The losses had been suffered due to beam attacks, the lack of cloud cover, the superior range of cannon, and fuel loss. To the sound of a shutting stable door, it was on the 18th that the Air Ministry ordered Bomber Command not to raid Heligoland again until each Wellington's tanks had been modified.

After 149 Squadron's survivors had been interrogated at Mildenhall – which would have made interesting listening – a party started in The Bird in the Hand, their local watering hole. Never had the beer been so welcome, enlivened by a laugh when they heard William Joyce, from Hamburg, claim that thirty-eight Wellingtons had been shot down. This from twenty-four despatched!

For Ruse and his fellow prisoners there was no rejoicing, just the hard reality of life behind bars in between bouts of interrogation by Luftwaffe officers who might be aggressive or charming, but whose motives remained the same. Stick to name, rank and number. The Germans would respect that, but say any more and attempts would be made to prise further details from you.

What was it that the Tangmere Spitfire boys had said after fighter affiliation? That they could destroy 37 Squadron in ten minutes? Nobody had believed them then.

Ludlow-Hewitt flew in to hear first-hand accounts, while other senior officers now accepted the need for beam guns and self-sealing tanks. However, even fifty-seven deaths did not quite mean the end of the self-defending bomber formation. It was noted that most of Kellett's formation had come home, whereas the others had not – something blamed on bad formation flying. Those now sitting in judgement still felt that their views on the subject were justified. It was easy to blame others who would never return. Despite this, Ludlow-Hewitt was right when he declared that the opposition on the 14th and 18th had been surprising. He correctly thought that crack squadrons had been brought in.

There were those below him, at some peril to their careers, who sought to get the message across. Flight Lieutenant Peter Grant, having nursed his damaged aircraft back to Honington, gave a lecture on daylight attacks at a Bomber Command gunnery school. Telling it like it was brought a reprimand for 'an unpatriotic talk likely to cause dismay and demoralisation'. Someone later realised he had told the truth, for he finished the war as a wing commander. Grant was one of the few survivors of that day to see peace again.

For others it was a short life in the fast lane. The following March, Flying Officer Bill Macrae and his crew flew in to Weybridge with another Wellington for tank modification, and were royally entertained there. Doubts were expressed as to their ability to fly back, but Macrae brushed these aside and took off. The Wellington turned steeply to port, dived and crashed on nearby St George's Hill, above an area known as the Sandpits. All five crew died.

Evidently some Whitehall warrior thought self-sealing tanks conferred immortality, for as 1940 dawned Paul Harris was ordered to send three Wellingtons on a daylight sweep over Heligoland. Up came I/ZG76's Bf 110s again and two more bombers went down.

At last the penny had started to drop. From now on most heavy bomber attacks would be by night, although the Air Ministry would never abandon the idea of daylight ones. 2 Group's Blenheims would continue these over Europe, with losses that abated somewhat when the superior Douglas Boston and the Mosquito came on the scene. For 3 Group the lesson had finally been learned, though it had cost too many lives to teach it.

10

CODEWORD DANZIG

At home that Christmas things went much as normal. For now there was still plenty of food in the shops, the only caution against indulgence being sounded by Sir John Simon, the Chancellor of the Exchequer, who contended that money should not be spent on presents. Few people paid any heed to him. The citizens of Birmingham continued to venture out despite the IRA making their presence felt with a series of bombs, the fourth of which wrecked a store in the city. Those who were still unemployed – all 1,270,000 of them – wondered if 1940 would bring any breaks.

On Christmas Day the time-honoured custom of making sure that all British servicemen – and now, women – received a Christmas dinner, wherever they were, was observed, often with officers acting as waiters. At three o'clock the King's speech was broadcast. He thanked the Navy and the RAF, with a special greeting to the BEF:

> Their task is hard. They are waiting, and waiting is a trial of nerve and discipline. But I know that when the moment comes for action they will prove themselves worthy of the highest traditions of their great Service. A new year is at hand. We cannot tell what it will bring. If it brings peace, how thankful we shall all be. If it brings us continued struggle we shall remain undaunted.

In Paris, too, Christmas continued in almost a pre-war atmosphere, with no food shortages. Maurice Chevalier or Josephine Baker entertained nightly at the Café de Paris. From the 1920s she had prospered in a country where, unlike her native America, skin colour mattered little.

Goebbels could not conceal a long face. The *Graf Spee*'s loss had not been easy to explain, coming as it did after what at first had seemed a German victory. Seeing the King's speech as 'sterile and idiotic', he declared, 'Although peace is the real meaning of Christmas, we shall talk peace only after victory.' Berlin's raffish nightlife continued, to his annoyance and to the delight of those in the capital who had long seen him as a narrow-minded, provincial little Rhinelander.

Hitler was out inspecting his front-line troops, some of them on French soil that Gamelin had abandoned in October. He spent Christmas Day with a Luftwaffe fighter unit and then with the List Regiment, with whom he had served in 1914–18. The German press hailed the fact that the Führer was with his men, unlike the Allied politicians.

⁕ ⁕ ⁕

During that winter Hitler spent much time at the Berghof, his home in the Obersalzberg mountains. Living up to their organisation's original function as the Führer's personal bodyguard, hundreds of SS men patrolled the area around it. Hitler habitually rose late, taking a walk after lunch. Planning meetings would take place from late in the afternoon until night, his maps being on a marble table by the Berghof's famous picture window.

In order that he should be close to what was to come, a new headquarters of four bunkers was being constructed for him, just 30 miles from the Belgian border. In keeping with Hitler's taste for the dramatic, it bore the codename *Felsennest* (eyrie).

His original plan, which would be put off no less than twenty-nine times by the bitter and long, drawn-out winter weather, was known by the codename *Fall Gelb* (Case Yellow). A heavy attack would take place in the north. All the armour would be concentrated in General von Bock's Army Group B, to cut through Belgium and Holland. Other groups, on the left under Generals von Leeb and von Rundsteht, would be there to support it:

> All available forces will be committed with the intention of bringing to battle on north French and Belgian soil as many sections of the French Army and its allies as possible. This will create favourable conditions for the future war against England and France on land and in the air.

On 21 October General Erich von Manstein, chief of staff to Army Group A, saw a copy of the plan, and voiced his disquiet. If Group B did swing through the Low Countries into Belgium, the result would be trench warfare all over again. Lacking sufficient motor transport, the General Staff had come up with a plan for only partial victory. They did not expect to conquer France with it, merely to grab the Channel coast in preparation for another long war. Von Manstein later commented, 'I found it humiliating, to say the least, that our generation could do nothing better than repeat an old recipe.'

He saw that Holland's many river obstacles would not make for good tank country. The dykes could be opened, bogging down the armour, while the areas around them had become more built-up over the past twenty years. These were not areas that tank crews cared to venture into, and with good reason. The 4th Panzer Division, in the Polish fighting, had lost fifty-seven tanks in Warsaw's suburbs. Consequently, von Manstein looked for a different route. If the armour went to Group A and through the Ardennes, once it had crossed the river Meuse, it would be able to deploy in the flat open country the crews liked.

Hitler too had been having second thoughts about the plan. On 29 October he amended it to leave Holland out, then the next day announced that he had had a brainwave for an attack through the Ardennes to strike at Sedan. Von Rundsteht, the commander of Army Group A, also wrote to his C-in-C, von Brauchitsch, explaining why the plan would not bring a decisive victory. Von Manstein suggested moving the armour from the north to the Ardennes. However, all this was seen as rivalry between the two army groups. Von Manstein's suggestions were filed away.

Not one to give up, von Manstein explained his ideas in detail when von Brauchitsch visited Group A's headquarters on 3 November. His C-in-C was not impressed, believing that *Fall Gelb* would take place long before there was any chance of changing it. However, things were beginning to go von Manstein's way. On 11 November, after another delay, Hitler ordered the XIX Panzerkorps to be redeployed to Group A, with Sedan as its objective. It was intended as no more than a diversion, the bulk of the armour still remaining in the north. General Heinz Guderian, in charge of this formation, agreed with von Manstein that a thrust through the Ardennes would be possible. As in the Polish campaign, Hitler was beginning to take a strong interest in every detail of the planning.

On 10 January Hitler gave the order for the attack to take place a week later, but it was on this day that an event occurred which in part expedited further changes. At a Luftwaffe base in Munster, Major Hellmuth Reinberger of the 7th Airborne Division complained of the uncomfortable train journey he faced to be at a staff meeting in Cologne the next day. Another major offered to fly him there in a communications aircraft. Strong winds and bad icing forced them down in a field near Malines, on the Belgian side of the border.

In the major's briefcase were operational orders for an airborne division at Cologne. By accepting the lift he had contravened orders that no secret papers were to be carried by air. With internment staring them in the face, and neither man a smoker, they borrowed a lighter from a Belgian peasant, but did not succeed in totally destroying their papers before gendarmes arrived.

What remained of the documents was passed to the Belgian High Command, who in a spirit of belated co-operation passed them on to the Allies. Although the Belgians took them seriously, neither Gamelin nor the BEF did, thinking them to be a plant. Nevertheless, despite von Rundstedt promptly reporting the matter in an attempt to force a change, things remained as they were for now. Army headquarters, seeing von Manstein as a troublemaker, exiled him to an infantry corps in eastern Germany.

The turning point finally came when von Manstein lunched with Hitler on 17 February. Afterwards, he explained his ideas in Hitler's study. This bold plan appealed to the Führer and fitted in with his own ideas. He was delighted that a professional should share them. It promised a blitzkrieg, not the war of attrition he had been dreading. Army headquarters, recognising which way the wind was now blowing, put forward a new plan which agreed with everything von Manstein had said, but gave him no credit for it. He remained in exile.

German cryptanalysts had broken French military codes the previous October. Their radio traffic showed that Sedan was held by two second-class French divisions. The revised plan was now set for 10 May. Spring weather would be no obstacle. The codeword would be *Danzig*.

11

THE FINAL MONTHS

At half past six on the morning of 3 February pairs of Heinkel 111s from KG26 took off from their temporary base in Schleswig at 3-minute intervals, tasked to intercept a British convoy southbound from the Swedish coast and thought to be currently off the English north-east coast. Any aircraft spotting it was to pass word to the others. One aircraft was flown by an all-Unteroffizier crew of four. The North Sea presented its customary grey and forbidding appearance, with snow flurries and mist that hung from the low cloud.

The only airfield in the north-east that was not snowbound was RAF Acklington in Northumberland. In its cold dispersal hut, on readiness, sat three pilots of 43 Squadron's B Flight – Flight Lieutenant Peter Townsend, Flying Officer 'Tiger' Folkes and Sergeant Jim Hallowes. Their Hurricanes waited outside.

Just after nine that morning the RDF operator at Danby Beacon, inland from Whitby, reported two unidentified aircraft 60 miles out, approaching at 1,000 feet. The three fighters were scrambled, and as Townsend headed south messages rasped in his ears. 'Vector 180. Bandits off Whitby. Angels one.' Then: 'Raiders attacking unarmed trawler off Whitby.'

Townsend saw the quarry first, but there was only one. There it was – the dark shape of a Heinkel, just below the cloud layer, above and to starboard of him, flying north-north-west. Townsend climbed to fire the opening burst, killing Rudolf Leuschake, the observer, in the bomber's nose as he shouted a warning. Smoke streamed from the starboard engine as Townsend banked away, with Folkes following him in to attack. Johan Meyer, manning the ventral gun, was mortally wounded in the stomach. In the dorsal position Karl Missy fired back desperately, his single gun totally outclassed by the eight guns of the three fighters. Then he was hit in the legs, leaving Hermann Wilms, the pilot, the only one not to be injured.

Wilms lifted the Heinkel into cloud, but realised that with failing power he could only go down, and who would survive a ditching in this weather? The coast was only 2 miles away. He emerged from the cloud, lowering the bomber's undercarriage – as much a sign of surrender as anything else – and headed towards Whitby, trailing a long plume of smoke.

People dashed into the streets below, amazed at the sight. There was the Heinkel, huge and pale blue overhead, with the Hurricanes hotly pursuing and still firing. Empty cartridge cases and belt links clattered into the streets around the harbour. The raider passed over Love Lane, to the west of the town, where Special Constable Arthur Barratt was at home with a cup of tea. Now it was down to 200 feet. Barratt leapt into his car and raced after it, turning right onto the Guisborough road.

Wilms desperately needed a landing space, but the snow-covered fields offered little that he could use. There was one, directly ahead, to the right of a main road, with houses by a T-junction. Down went the Heinkel, its wheels collapsing as it ran up the field towards a line of sycamore trees leading away from the road. In a shower of snow and mud, it ploughed its way across a narrow lane, stopping just behind the houses.

The scene was described by PC Barratt in an understandably excited letter to his brother the next day:

As soon as I saw what the result of the battle was going to be I dashed for my car and was up past Sneaton Castle before the snow settled down when he hit the ground, and reached him just as he came to rest. I, along with some farm chaps, dashed up to him and I climbed on to the wing. The first Englishman to enter a German plane landing in England since the war started.

When I looked into the cockpit what a sight met my eyes. The Pilot was kneeling down in the bottom of the plane burning his papers, with two of his mates leaning against him, moaning and groaning. I got hold of his collar and pulled him off his papers, but he got clear of me and finished his job of work before I could get to him again. (I was hanging head down in the cockpit.)

An unforgettable visitor, photographed from the lane leading to Bannial Flat Farm. (*After The Battle*)

Wilms then fired a Very flare into the shattered nose, but this attempt to destroy the Heinkel's remains failed. The dead man and his two injured comrades were removed, the latter going to Whitby Hospital, which by now was getting used to dealing with wounded enemy airmen. Meyer died later that day and Missy suffered a leg amputation.

Although 43 Squadron celebrated that evening, Townsend's sensitive nature led him to think of the Heinkel's crew. When the news of what had happened to Missy and Meyer reached him, he travelled to Whitby the next day.

Townsend and Missy did not speak each other's language, but the look they exchanged made no words necessary. Despite Missy's weakness, he clasped Townsend's hand hard. His eyes, Townsend said later, reminded him of a wounded animal. A bag of oranges and cigarettes was handed over, then Townsend left, never to forget what he had just seen.

The snow did not deter the souvenir hunters. Here was a Heinkel to rival the Humbie one. One of them was Wilf McNeil, of the Observer Corps and well known as a blacksmith at Pickering, 20 miles away. Many years later he showed me the small piece of metal he retrieved, believing it to be part of the bomber's aileron linkage. Whitby's Pannett Park Museum includes a diorama of the crash scene.

Rudolf Leuschake and Johan Meyer were buried in a plot at Catterick, accompanied by a wreath that read 'From 43 Squadron, with sympathy'. Any ideas of burying them locally were dropped due to angry feelings about airmen who attacked fishing vessels. In 1943 Missy was repatriated in a POW exchange.

Today the houses so nearly demolished that snowy morning still stand by the junction of the Guisborough and Pickering roads, now next to a small traffic island. A plaque nearby commemorates what happened, but it may be asked how many of today's motorists, hurrying past, have time to take note of it.

On 9 February KG26 lost another Heinkel, this time from their 5th Staffel, to 602 Squadron's CO, Squadron Leader Farquhar. One man died and three others were taken prisoner when their aircraft force-landed at North Berwick Law in East Lothian. A moderately good forced landing on its wheels resulted in very little damage, even though the bomber finished up on its nose. Consequently it was repaired and flown south from Turnhouse to Farnborough with an escort of Hurricanes. Repainted in RAF colours and given the serial number AW177, it was the first aircraft to join 1426 (Enemy Aircraft Circus) Flight, which went round Allied airfields showing captured types to those likely to meet them in action.

Throughout these months the leaflet raids had continued, as if doing so would incite the Germans to rise up and overthrow their despotic government. Not all the paper went to them, however. On the night of 15/16 March, 77 Squadron's Whitleys went to Warsaw. One of them nearly

Squadron Leader Farquhar's victim nosed over at North Berwick on 9 February 1940.
(IWM Neg. No. HU58526)

did not return. Its story is told here in a contemporary account by the BBC journalist Charles Gardner:

The pilots – one a flight lieutenant and the other a flying officer – were in a British bomber which had been night flying. On the way back they ran into a strong headwind and had to climb to 18,000 feet over a layer of cloud; the climbing and the headwind took up a lot of petrol, with the result that they began to run short. It was still dark, but they decided that they were certain to be over French territory, so they came down through the clouds – which incidentally were on the hill tops – and circled round at five hundred feet. They could see one or two villages and a town with factory chimneys, a place they estimated of about 25,000 inhabitants.

Then, as our plane was looking for a field, an anti-aircraft gun fired a warning shot, so the flight lieutenant put on his navigation lights, gave a recognition signal, and put down his wheels – and there was no more firing. Still thinking he was over France, the pilot chose his field and landed in it, unloaded the plane's guns, stopped the engines and, with the flying officer, got out of the machine. At the other end of the field they could see a group of peasants running towards them and they went out to meet them, which they did about two hundred yards from the plane. The flying officer spoke to the leader of the peasant group and said chattily, 'C'est France, n'est pas?' The peasant just looked at him, and shook his head. The flying officer tried again and said encouragingly, 'Luxembourg alors?' Another head-shake, but this time the peasant pointed to one of his friends and said, 'Hans Franzoisch', meaning that Hans spoke French. To which he replied in a strong German accent, but very politely, 'Non, Monsieur, c'est l'Allemagne, la frontière est à vingt kilometres,' and obligingly he pointed out the direction in which the frontier lay.

Flight Lieutenant Tomalin and his crew ran back to the Whitley. It was as well that Merlin engines started easily. They took off again just as German troops started running from the far end of the field. They fired without hitting the bomber, which landed at the French airfield of Villeneuve with tanks almost dry, though not before checking a hoarding advertising a French drink, just to be sure. Afterwards Gardner's report and the newsreel commentator made it all seem a joke, but it could have turned out very differently.

Shipping attacks were not confined to the east coast. The steamer SS *Barn Hill* was en route for London from Halifax, Nova Scotia, when she was attacked 3 miles off Beachy Head on the evening of 20 March.

Flight Lieutenant Tomalin and his crew – with the only Whitley to land in Germany and return. (IWM Neg. No. C1011)

A stick of bombs straddled the vessel, one killing four of her crew when it started a fire in the No. 4 hold, which contained rubber and carbide. A distress call resulted in a Dutch vessel taking off eighteen of the *Barn Hill*'s crew, but for some reason the Coastguard delayed calling out the Eastbourne lifeboat *Jane Holland* until 45 minutes after the attack.

By the time the lifeboat reached the scene, the *Barn Hill* was drifting, experiencing a series of explosions. Having taken off what appeared to be all the survivors, including the eighteen previously rescued, the lifeboat returned to shore. However, it became clear that six men, including the skipper, were unaccounted for. The crew of a Newhaven tug, the *Foremost*, had come alongside and been surprised to hear the ship's bell ringing. Through the wreckage on deck they could see a man gripping the bell's rope between his teeth.

To get closer would have placed the tug and its crew in danger, so the *Jane Holland* was called out again. Two volunteers, lifeboatmen Alec F. Huggett and Thomas Allchorn, climbed on board and picked their way through the wreckage, while the tug's crew played a hose on the fires around them. The bell's ringer turned out to be the skipper, Captain O'Neil, who had sustained multiple injuries when he had been blown from the bridge onto the foredeck.

Having taken the captain to hospital ashore, the *Jane Holland* returned again, this time with some of the Eastbourne Fire Brigade on board. From the seafront hundreds of spectators watched as the blazing ship was run aground at Langney Point. Two days later the *Barn Hill* broke her back, scattering her cargo onto the adjacent beaches. A great deal of unofficial salvage followed, the locals supplementing their rations with whatever was in the tins with which they waded ashore. As the labels had been washed off, only sloshing the tin's contents back and forth gave any clue as what they might be. The courage of Alec Huggett and Thomas Allchorn was recognised by the award of the RNLI's Bronze Medal.

The 3rd of April dawned grey and overcast. It may have presented no problems to the Yorkshire coast's fishermen, but at Catterick there was some debate as to whether a patrol should be mounted when, according to the pilots' saying, even the birds were walking. One that was not was a Heinkel 111 reported attacking shipping 4 miles north of Whitby.

By now a grass airstrip at Greatham, renamed RAF West Hartlepool, had become a satellite of Catterick, and it was from there that Flight Lieutenant Norman Ryder was scrambled. The Heinkel was another from KG26, this time commanded by the Gruppenkommandeur, Oberstleutnant Hans Hefele, with four other crew, on an armed reconnaissance against British shipping. These flights' timing was such that several aircraft simultaneously arrived in different places over the North Sea, thus splitting up any fighter defence. A low cloud base was necessary, and flying over Britain was still forbidden.

Spotting a small convoy, they attacked the largest vessel, but were hit in turn by return fire in the port engine and wing. Leutnant Rudolf Behnisch, the pilot, could no longer change the pitch of the port propeller, which slowed him down, and suction from the wing flak hole caused the aircraft to drift to port. Attempts to re-trim it and get the crew to pump fuel from the port wing tanks to the starboard ones were set at naught when his wireless operator, Unteroffizier Albert Weber, called out, 'British fighter plane approaching from behind!'

Ryder had already seen that his quarry was in trouble. It was now flying so slowly that he had to throttle back, passing ahead in a circle before attacking from behind. Before he could do so, Hefele, lying in the nose, fired at him. Ryder knew his engine had been hit, but moments later a 6-second burst from his own guns put the starboard engine out. He refrained from a second attack when he saw it stream smoke and flame.

All this was watched by the crew of a Scarborough drifter, the *Silver Line*. Her skipper, Bill Watkinson, had been dive-bombed three weeks before and although he had taken no hits, this time his brother Tom was ready behind the Lewis gun they carried. Now, as the Heinkel approached it collected another burst, wounding Leutnant Georg Kempe, the observer, in the head.

The bomber ditched in a watery cascade, its crew scrambling onto a wing but finding their dinghy bullet-holed and useless. Ryder circled overhead, waving in salute and Behnisch noted the Spitfire was trailing white fluid. That meant a punctured glycol tank. Like all liquid-cooled designs, the Rolls-Royce Merlin was vulnerable to overheating caused by loss of coolant. No coolant, no engine.

As the drifter headed towards them the Heinkel dipped beneath the waves, casting its crew into the sea, but for the moment its tail was still visible, rearing up like that of a whale. Behnisch, with a damaged lifejacket, hung onto it until *Silver Line* was close enough. Ropes came flying over and the Germans scrambled thankfully aboard. A rifle-waving crewman made sure that a pistol carried by one of them was promptly handed over.

Docile, but wondering what kind of reception they would receive, the Germans relaxed when the crew told them they would be well treated as prisoners. Hefele then said, 'Make for England. We never wanted to fight you anyway!' Perhaps that was said in an attempt to better their chances, but it is curious to note that it came after Hochstuhl's similar comment at Sandsend the previous October. Would their attitude have been different if they had gone straight on to fight the Soviet Union? Certainly their fate would have been. The crew received a watch and signet ring as a thank-you.

Now Ryder also faced a ditching. Even as he called his control to advise them of his situation, the oil gauge temperature was rising alarmingly, accompanied by hot glycol fumes in the cockpit. By now he was 15 miles out to sea off the town of Redcar, but clearly he was not going to make it.

Too low to bale out, he circled the trawler *Alaskan* and decided to ditch close to her. As he slid open the hood at 50 feet, his engine failed.

The sudden deceleration in water threw him forward, knocking him unconscious. He came to only as cold water splashed over him. Opening his eyes, he found he was already under water – green water that was rapidly darkening. Pulling out the harness quick-release pin, he stood up but was still not free – his parachute had caught under the cockpit hood. His mouth full of salty water, he struggled free, splashing to the surface.

Even now he might not survive, for the chute was a heavy burden, dragging him through the waves instead of over them. With what seemed like the last of his strength, he turned the harness release to the left and banged it. The chute came away and as it did so he realised it had been the one thing keeping him afloat, for his lifejacket would not inflate. Desperately he grabbed the chute again. Then the trawler was there, with shouts coming from above him. Something touched his arm, he grabbed it and felt other arms lifting him.

Ryder went to Hartlepool, returning to the officers' mess at Catterick with quite a tale to tell. His description of the darkening sea earned him the nickname 'Green to Black'. The *Alaskan*'s skipper, Bill Caske, was later presented with an engraved tankard by 41 Squadron. Ryder's Spitfire was the first home defence fighter lost to enemy action.

The Germans were landed at Scarborough, where a waiting ambulance took Kempe to hospital. The rest were fed at the police station before going to the Army's Burniston Barracks. Three days later the *Silver Line*'s crew were received at the town hall, where the mayor presented a silver statuette of a lifeboatman to each of them. Afterwards they visited Kempe, presenting him with cigarettes and oranges, the latter by now a scarce commodity. Humanity still ruled, despite this war's demands.

✳   ✳   ✳

From the beginning of 1940 German Intelligence had reported that Churchill was seeking permission from the Cabinet to mine Norwegian territorial waters. It was another reason why Hitler had ordered his OKW Operations Staff to prepare *Studie Nord* – an invasion plan for Norway and possibly Denmark.

The Allies were planning two operations, the first being to lay two minefields off Norway, with a third marked, but not laid, as a deterrent. It was assumed that the Germans would react with a seaborne invasion, which would be dealt with by the Home Fleet. An Anglo-French force would then occupy Narvik, seizing the railway to the Swedish iron ore fields. It was further assumed that the Norwegians would not resist and that any German reaction would not be strong. Hitler would not have sufficient resources to fight in Scandinavia and on the Western Front simultaneously. Even Chamberlain seemed confident, declaring 'Hitler has missed the bus!' It was a remark he would soon regret.

Tension was rising in Scandinavia. At the end of March 1940 the Swiss Ambassador in Stockholm informed his government that Allied and German landings in Norway were imminent. This was intercepted by the German listening service. Then the Finnish Ambassador in Paris repeated a remark by the French Premier concerning the British mining plan.

Hitler's plan, brought in over the heads of his Service chiefs, was a bold one. Daring and seamanship were demanded from the Kriegsmarine. They were to steam into Norwegian ports to disembark assault troops. Paratroops would be supported by infantry flown in by Ju 52s, escorted by Luftwaffe fighters, to capture Norwegian airfields. Their initial targets would be Oslo, Stavanger, Kristiansand, Bergen, Trondheim and Narvik.

Success would depend on darkness. Grossadmiral Raeder suggested 7 April as an ideal date, for there would be no moon that night. Hitler gave his approval, but moved the date of landing in Norway to the 9th. Security was tight until the last minute; although crews' shore leave was suddenly cancelled on the 6th, as they reported back aboard few had any idea where they were going. Landings at different points had to be co-ordinated, and had to include a rising by Quisling's fifth columnists.

Vizeadmiral Günther Lütjens would command that part of the fleet detailed for Narvik and Trondheim, from the battlecruiser *Gneisenau*. On the afternoon of the 6th he briefed all his officers in her wardroom. Shortly afterwards an order of the day from Raeder reached all the ships involved:

> Success will be ours if every leader realises the magnitude of his task and knows how to surmount the difficulties. We cannot foresee the immediate outcome of these events, or the ultimate consequences. But experience tells us that success always favours those who are ready to accept responsibility and who act boldly with tenacity and skill.

Three hundred miles of sea lay ahead, from which the Home Fleet could strike at any time. A casualty rate of 50 per cent was considered acceptable – acceptable, that is, to those who would not be there on the day. Events were now moving to an inevitable climax.

It was not as if the Allies did not know they were out of harbour. Air reconnaissance had revealed an empty anchorage at Wilhelmshaven, and after the fleet moved off before dawn on the 7th twelve Blenheims attacked it in the Skagerrak. They met heavy fire and no bombs hit. Another attack by Wellingtons scored no hits either.

On this date an agent's report of enemy intentions reached London. It was seen as 'of doubtful value and may well only be a further move in the war of nerves'. That evening the Home Fleet put to sea, but the Admiralty considered the German movements to be an attempted breakout into the

Atlantic. Consequently any chance to attack the invasion force before it reached Norway was missed.

Lütjens had hoped for foul weather, but it had been fair initially, aiding the RAF in their attacks. Now it deteriorated, rising to a Force 10 gale, spreading seasickness among the mountain troops crammed onto the destroyers. Heavy seas washed boats and some of their vehicles overboard. One man followed them, but there was no turning back for him. Lütjens was determined to keep to the schedule, ordering a speed of 26 knots. The destroyers, less able to ride the heavy seas, fell back, but Lütjens ordered their commanders to close up at first light.

It was on the 8th that Operation *Wilfred* – the planned mining of Norwegian waters – finally went ahead, the battlecruiser *Renown* adding heavy punch to a force that included the destroyer HMS *Glowworm*. Having turned about when she lost a man overboard, *Glowworm* suddenly met the German destroyer *Bernd von Arnim*, whose call for assistance brought the heavy cruiser *Admiral Hipper* to the scene. Faced with this monster, *Glowworm* defiantly rammed the cruiser, then turned over and sank.

Despite 500 tons of water in her bows, *Hipper* turned with her destroyer escort, resuming her course for Trondheim. By the evening of the 8th the weather had abated, enabling hot meals to be served to soldiers and sailors alike, which raised morale. *Scharnhorst* and *Gneisenau*, acting as decoys to draw off the Home Fleet, traded salvoes with *Renown* in a snowstorm, each causing some damage to the other.

When news of the invasion broke, Churchill declared in the House of Commons, 'In my view, which is shared by my skilled advisers, Herr Hitler has committed a grave strategic error.'

They were wrong. Allied efforts to intervene were muddled from the start. Army units were loaded onto ships, offloaded, then put back on again. Some went into action without vital equipment or any training in winter warfare. The result was a confused two-month battle among the mountains and fjords. German newsreels showed sullen men in muddy battledress being led away into captivity. Ahead of them lay five years behind the wire. The Royal Navy played its part to the full, both in landing troops and evacuating them, but finally learned to its cost that operating warships close inshore without air superiority was asking for defeat.

Bomber Command attacked shipping in the Stavanger area by day, finally ditching the idea of the self-defending bomber formation when nine Wellingtons and Hampdens were lost, mostly to fighter attack. Fighter pilots sent to Norway did their best with a handful of Hurricanes and Gladiators. The wreck of one, later salvaged from a Norwegian lake and now on display in the RAF Museum at Hendon, sums up what they had to face. En route to Norway the Germans also invaded Denmark, which fell in a day with little resistance.

The Kriegsmarine did not have things all their own way, losing three cruisers and ten destroyers, but the Germans got what they came for – the continuation of the iron ore supply and new bases from which to attack Britain.

While all this was going on, the assumption that Hitler could not fight on two fronts was disproved. On Friday 10 May, as planned, *Fall Gelb* went ahead. Allied aircraft were bombed on the ground, with those of Holland and Belgium, whose neutrality was ruthlessly violated. Holland fell in four days and Belgium succumbed soon after. The AASF's Battles were chopped from the sky and Allied troop movements were hampered by fleeing refugees. The French line broke at Sedan and German armour surged across flat country, its crews as surprised as anyone else by the speed of their success.

A new era had begun, with no more talk of phoney wars.

*   *   *

Today in the London area there are two reminders of that period in Britain's history. One is the cruiser HMS *Belfast*, veteran of Arctic convoys, the Battle of North Cape, D-Day and the Korean War. Aboard her is the first magnetic mine defused at Shoeburyness.

The other reminder is N2980, a Wellington Mark IA. This aircraft served with 149 Squadron in 1939, surviving the Heligoland Bight raid on

Ouvry's mine is today displayed aboard HMS *Belfast*. (Author's collection)

18 December. Following an engine failure during a training flight on New Year's Eve 1940, it ditched in Loch Ness, sinking while its last two crew members paddled ashore in the dinghy. In 1985 it was recovered, in pieces, and the painstaking process of reassembling it began close to the factory at Weybridge in which it had been built.

This bomber, fully assembled and partly re-skinned, now forms part of the displays at Brooklands Museum. It serves to remind people that Bomber Command's force did not consist solely of Lancasters and Mosquitoes.

People flocked to see this Loch Ness monster every time a BBC documentary on it was shown, and it became part of my job there to conduct tours around the hangar that still houses it. One I shall never forget concerned a gentleman whose brother had died on the Heligoland Bight raid. I took him in to see what then were silver skeletal remains, chose my words carefully, then stepped back to allow a moment of silence.

I did not have to look at him to know what he was thinking. Why did this aircraft return that day, and not my brother's?

Why indeed?

APPENDIX

SHIPPING LOSSES TO MINES LAID BY U-BOATS

September 1939 – April 1940

Name	Nationality	Date	Laid by
Magdapur	British	10/09/39	*U-13*
Goodwood	British	10/09/39	*U-15*
Alex van Opstal	Belgian	15/09/39	*U-26*
Orsa	British	21/09/39	*U-15*
City of Paris	British	16/10/39	*U-13*
Capitaine Edmond Laborie	French	21/10/39	*U-19*
Deodata	Norwegian	21/10/39	*U-19*
Konstantinos Hadjipateras	Greek	24/10/39	*U-19*
Phryne	British	24/10/39	*U-13*
Carmarthen Coast	British	09/11/39	*U-24*
Carica Milica	Yugoslavian	18/11/39	*U-19*
Sainte Clair	French	20/11/39	*U-16*
Elena R	Greek	22/11/39	*U-26*
Ionian	British	29/11/39	*U-20*
Washington	British	06/12/39	*U-59*
Willowpool	British	10/12/39	*U-20*
Marwick Head	British	12/12/39	*U-59*
City of Kobe	British	19/12/39	*U-60*
Mars	Swedish	20/12/39	*U-22*
Resercho	British	21/12/39	*U-15*
Glen Albyn	British	23/12/39	*U-31*
Promotive	British	23/12/39	*U-31*
Loch Donn	British	25/12/39	*U-22*
Stanholme	British	25/12/39	*U-33*
Hanne	Danish	28/12/39	*U-22*
El Oso	British	11/01/40	*U-30*
Inverdargle	British	16/01/40	*U-33*
Caroni River	British	20/01/40	*U-34*
Protosilaus	British	21/01/40	*U-28*
Ferry Hill	British	21/01/40	*U-61*
Eston	British	28/01/40	*U-22*
Anu	Estonian	06/02/40	*U-13*
Munster	British	07/02/40	*U-30*
Chagres	British	09/02/40	*U-30*

Royal Archer	British	24/02/40	*U-21*
Cato	British	03/03/40	*U-29*
Counsellor	British	08/03/40	*U-32*

This list does not include damaged ships, or those lost to mines laid by surface ships and aircraft. An absence of losses during April 1940 shows that by then U-boats had been taken off this work for the Norwegian campaign. The list was compiled with the assistance of Peter Sharpe's book *U-boat Fact File*.

During the period September 1939 – April 1940, 214 British ships, 29 Allied and 190 neutral ones were lost, making a total of 433. I am grateful to fellow author Ben Carver for this information.

GLOSSARY

Every war produces jargon and this one was no exception. Translations of German ranks are also given.

AA	Anti-aircraft
AFC	Air Force Cross
AFV	Armoured fighting vehicle
AOC	Air Officer Commanding
CB	Companion of the Bath
CO	Commanding Officer
DFC	Distinguished Flying Cross
DSM	Distinguished Service Medal
DSO	Distinguished Service Order
ENSA	Entertainments National Services Association, nicknamed 'Every Night Something Awful'
Gefreiter	Lance Corporal
Grossadmiral	Admiral of the Fleet
Hauptmann	Captain (Army or Air Force)
IFF	Identification Friend or Foe – a device fitted to friendly aircraft that changed the shape of their blip on an RDF screen
JG	Jagdgeschwader (Fighter Group)
Kapitän zur See	Captain (Navy)

Kapitänleutnant	Lieutenant
KCB	Knight Commander of the Bath
KG	Kampfgeschwader (Bomber Group)
Korvettenkapitän	Lieutenant Commander
Kriegsmarine	German Navy
LAC	Leading aircraftman
Leutnant	Second lieutenant
Luftwaffe	German Air Force
MC	Military Cross
Oberfeldwebel	Sergeant Major
Oberleutnant	Lieutenant
OKW	Oberkommando der Wehrmacht (Headquarters of the German Armed Forces)
RAAF	Royal Australian Air Force
RDF	Radio Direction Finding, to become radar
SAP	Semi-armour piercing
Schwarme	Formation of four aircraft
Staffelkapitän	Leader of a staffel (equivalent to an RAF squadron)
Unteroffizier	Corporal
Vizeadmiral	Vice Admiral
Waafs	Members of the Women's Auxiliary Air Force
W/T	Wireless Telegraphy
ZG	Zestörergeschwader (Destroyer Fighter Group)

ACKNOWLEDGEMENTS

The idea for this book dates back to the autumn of 1981, when I travelled on a battlefield tour that took in the Maginot Line forts at Hackenberg and Immerdorf, in the company of a BEF veteran who had served in that area during 1939–40.

It took a further step forward when, during a search for the Loch Ness Monster, a Wellington bomber was found and salvaged in 1985. This focused my attention on Brooklands Museum, where I later had the pleasure of meeting Sir George Edwards. His account of how the mine-clearing Wellington came about was told, with remarkable recall long after the event, in a typically down-to-earth style.

My thanks go, once again, to the National Archives staff at Kew and at the Imperial War Museum's Department of Photographs for their patient assistance. The account of HMS *Royal Oak*'s sinking was in part taken from the research of James Hayward, Alexander McKee, David Turner and Nigel West. Chapter 9 owes much to the thoroughly researched book *The Battle Of Heligoland Bight*, by Robin Holmes. Len Deighton's book *Blitzkrieg* gave further details from the German point of view. Bill Norman's two books on the Luftwaffe over northern England caused me to look at my home ground with new eyes.

If I have achieved anything, it is to put these stories and others together, presenting Britain's efforts during the first few months by sea, land and air, as well as depicting the impact on people who had once thought that such things could never recur. In so doing I was struck by how, three times over, the same situation occurred. Each of Britain's Services had become complacent after 1918, underfunded later, then hamstrung by obsolete equipment and outdated ideas when war returned. That Britain survived in 1940 seems all the more miraculous.

Stephen Flower
April 2011

INDEX

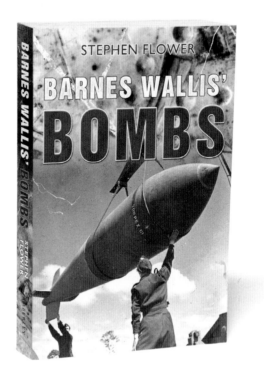

Barnes Wallis' Bombs
Stephen Flower

Barnes Wallis was the most famous inventor and designer of the Second World War. His story is not just of the 'bouncing' bombs that destroyed the Möhne and Eder dams but also of the other devices he invented, from the Wellington bomber to the Tallboy and Grand Slam bombs that this book is about.

Wallis was one of the most prolific inventors of armaments during the war, and his Highball, Upkeep and Tallboy bombs, as well as the truly massive Grand Slam earthquake bombs, helped to destroy such high-profile targets as the Bielefeld viaduct and led to the eventual sinking of the German battleship Tirpitz. His bombs were only eclipsed in destructive power by the atom bombs dropped on Hiroshima and Nagasaki in August 1945.

Stephen Flower's interest in Barnes Wallis' bombs and the men who dropped them on Nazi-occupied Europe began when he worked at Brooklands, home of Vickers, which built the Wellington, and where Wallis had his design office.

Paperback
384 pages
ISBN: 978-1-84868-959-6
£19.99

www.amberleybooks.com